PRAISE FOR *THE WOMEN'S BOOK OF EMPOWERMENT*

"When we are constantly aware of the Divine within, finding life's goodness becomes automatic. In any situation, we can be thankful and view life through a joyful lens, which is a core message of this book."

> – Lynn A. Robinson, author of *Divine Intuition* and *Real Prosperity*

"A handy resource to quickly experience a more productive and sensible way to view the world."

> – Arielle Ford, author of *Hot Chocolate for the Mystical Soul*

"*The Women's Book of Empowerment* is a gift for those who help others develop conscious awareness. It is a tremendous tool for those who mend the spirit because it guides people away from old, outdated ideas that no longer foster their self-development."

> – Lance Secretan, PhD, author of *Inspire! What Great Leaders Do* and *Inspirational Leadership: Destiny, Calling and Cause*

"An affirmation a day will bring your inner Goddess out to play."

> – Rev. Laurie Sue Brockway, author of *A Goddess Is a Girl's Best Friend: A Divine Guide to Find Love, Success and Happiness* and *Wedding Goddess: A Divine Guide to Transforming Wedding Stress into Wedding Bliss*

THE WOMEN'S BOOK
OF EMPOWERMENT

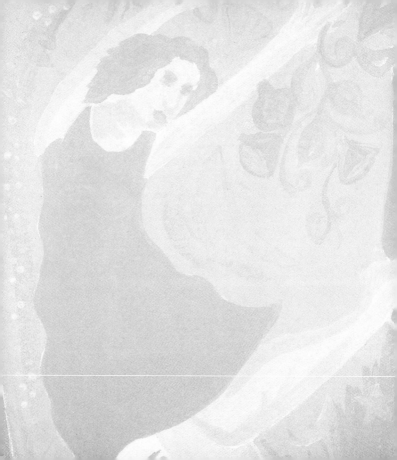

THE
WOMEN'S
BOOK OF
EMPOWERMENT

*323 Affirmations That Change
Everyday Problems
into Moments of Potential*

CHARLENE M. PROCTOR, PhD

First Paperback Edition 2005

Printed in Canada

ISBN 0-9766012-1-4

Library of Congress Control Number
2005922998

Published by The Goddess Network Press,
Birmingham, Michigan
Member of the Divine Mother's Light
Deployment Team

www.thegoddessnetwork.net

The Goddess Network® and The Goddess
Network Press® are registered trademarks
of The Goddess Network, Inc.

For information on special discounts for
bulk purchases of this book, please contact
The Goddess Network at 1-866-888-4633
or tgn@thegoddessnetwork.net.

Cover design by Cattails Multimedia Inc.
Original illustrations by Louise Hopson
Text design by Counterpunch/Peter Ross

To women everywhere
who know the power is within
to change your world:
this book is for you.

CONTENTS

Balance: Affirmations that help manage the
daily complexity of work, family, and you

Abundance: Affirmations that help you create
a mental equivalent to manifest what you desire

INTRODUCTION

Every day we have an opportunity to choose our attitude and focus our intentions in the present moment. Because of this choice, our own personal lives and all that we see in the world originate within the mind. Our physical experience is our 360-degree review on how we think. Put simply, our job is to fully participate in life but be consciously aware of what we want to create. Then we can look at the results and make adjustments. This is what it's like to have an empowered life. And to do this, we must first know that life is a cooperative arrangement between us and a divine presence we call God. We're all in it together, thinking certain thoughts and making choices that eventually become reality: a real-life reflection of our own thoughts.

To realize this power, with strength and self-confidence, we must also embrace spirit by recognizing that this strength lives within each and every one of us *today*. I call it our God-self. It is that spark of divine energy that constitutes our unique and beautiful selves. So the strength to create comes from making choices based in the present moment, not as a reaction to events, relationships, or experiences from long ago that no longer matter. Deciding to live in the present is the key to an empowered life. It is our gift from God. And it's a choice we have the freedom to make.

The evidence of these truths rests in our *ability* to create a life we desire. But harnessing this capacity to live consciously and presently takes a great deal of focus and a lot of practice. We must especially believe that we *are* powerful and filled with our God-selves. Because we are part of the Divine, we are divine as well. We do, in fact, co-create our world and accept responsibility for what we are about to learn.

Why is this outlook so difficult for people to embrace? Well, it's not easy to be a co-creator with God in a world that appears to be filled with noise and negativity, so we lose our focus and intentions easily. Judging from the media's appetite for disaster and worst-case scenarios, even our culture does not reward present-moment awareness or positive thinking; it pushes that responsibility onto someone or something else. And it seems we're always dredging up the past or preparing for catastrophe.

Now, more than ever, we are being nudged by the universe to arrive at the realization that life is so very much more than what we see. Science, medicine, and mystics have finally joined forces to confirm what we suspected: when the brain-body-heart composite is fully operational, using our capabilities to the largest degree possible, we *can* manifest our most positive thoughts into forms of happiness, prosperity, or jobs we love. *Our power to create reality lies within us.* We *can* make positive change. It is our birthright, our God-self put into motion, that gives us the opportunity to illuminate others by creative design. And by claiming responsibility for what we create, we in turn are allowed to grow and self-develop.

Life, seen from this perspective, is a giant learning laboratory where constant feedback is provided from our personal expression, testing and expanding our limits, evaluating what works and what doesn't. So at the day's end we're all scientists: data gatherers and mini-creators interacting within this rich environment, a continuum of ideas from the past in hand, understanding more about what we can do today and tomorrow for our own self-development. It's an amazing learning opportunity. The complexity and genius of this program, all for our benefit, is enough to validate our importance. We are significant, each and every one of us, because we are all helping to evolve our souls and the collective consciousness, which, simply put, is everyone's state of mind and heart. It is made up of our thoughts, our prayers, and our dreams for the future, and the love we have for others.

The journey of becoming a conscious observer, or pursuing a state of awareness about how you think, is itself a valuable experience. Because this existence has undulating characteristics, some divinely inspired as well as a number of the more conventional human brand, we are unlikely to get our minds in the right place the first time. Often, we learn from the trial and error of arranging a combination of emotions and thoughts around a set of ideas that create a reality. And to arrive with imagination, you need to be focused and love what you believe in. Clarity and interest, as Emmet Fox used to say, are what we need to establish an intention that attracts what we desire. He called it a mental equivalent. You must know what you want and have a passion for it.

Negative thoughts and old patterns of thinking prevent us from offering the world our special talents and doing the work we love, which can be anything from managing a home or a family to running a Fortune 500 company. Having the discipline to choose our thoughts is also a challenge, especially when old baggage gets in the way. Our day unfolds with surprises, both good and bad, but on a good day, we are able to embrace life at all levels of experience and move forward with a sense of accomplishment. On the bad days, we must deeply believe that the very core of our spirit is waiting to be put to good use, then go to bed, get up, and just try something different.

Changing our perception of worldly experiences is the only way to separate the concept of failure from our vocabulary and substitute a language of success and learning. You are brave for being on this planet during such difficult times. Remember, your soul chose to be here to test your human capabilities to make change in the most arduous circumstances. There is no failure, only a greater opportunity to put your God-self to work. That includes taking charge of your destiny and ending the self-blame for past experiences that no longer have any bearing upon what you can accomplish today.

Since I wrote *Let Your Goddess Grow! 7 Spiritual Lessons*

on *Female Power and Positive Thinking*, I have helped men and women change their minds to create more harmony and abundance. Many people tell me they've trained themselves to process life very differently; some even admit that negative thinking is just a bad habit. Others had unconsciously assumed ownership of old hurts left over from parents and institutions, such as guilt and unforgiveness; they were unaware of old mental programming which translated into heartache, careers they did not like, or near-bankruptcy. When you start taking inventory, it's amazing how often we keep wounds open from situations that no longer matter. We discover that those wounds are really the foundation upon which we have built negative and unproductive states of living for ourselves.

How can we alter our course to reset our thinking to the self-empowerment zone on the dial? To feel productive and balanced, we can develop *conscious awareness* of those thought patterns that prevent us from expressing our gifts.

With a little self-discipline, we can begin to reveal our divine selves, letting our light blast forth with no inhibitions and no agenda beyond the simple purpose of evolving our souls with as much zest as possible. When that happens, life suddenly moves from struggle to joy.

We must also identify with the source of our power, which is the Divine, and attach our self-image to emotions, the most important of which is love. It's how we get things done the right way. It is how we discover our *true selves*, our spirit-power awaiting recognition. When we honor the Divine within us, we no longer wait for life to begin; we jump-start it all on our own. And women, as a unique subset of the population of soul seekers, need to realize that the Divine seeks expression *through* us. Women have the same spirit-power as men and should be marvelously unrestrained in letting it loose. When it comes to working in this Department of Divine Power, the glorious, beloved female is eminently qualified.

By participating in life this way, both men and women

are channels of the spiritual source. Once we resonate with that idea, our short time on earth will be spent cultivating circumstances that reflect who we are, both within and outside organizations and families. We'll resonate with values that make sense, and we'll attract goodness. We will move toward a more meaningful existence.

How to Use *The Women's Book of Empowerment*

A positive, affirmative statement is a declaration to the universe that you choose to take the upper hand and never accept anything less than what you deserve. Affirmations are always made in the present tense, and they train the mind to stay in the present moment. They help you arrest the impulse to self-doubt and give you more energy to focus your attention on a life filled with prosperity, love, good health, and happiness.

When you release a negative thought, the goal is to

make peace with your situation – permanently – instead of rehashing the bad stuff. In this way, you will reverberate with love, not fear, and invite more wonder into your life. At that moment, you will have accepted the greatest and most complete vision of who you are: an empowered and marvelous spark of the Divine.

The affirmations in this book are arranged into seven power lessons and many categories of everyday problems. If you find yourself on the downward spiral of self-doubt and discouragement, and you're not sure where to find what you're experiencing, look in the table of contents. It lists challenges women frequently encounter, leading them to accumulate huge résumés of negativity and stress. Retrain your mind to reprogram your response to that stress. Find an affirmation, read it, repeat it, and take a moment to affirm what good you can find in the challenge. If you use these affirmations in conjunction with the spiritual lessons found in *Let Your Goddess Grow!* you will be able to make more room in your life for imagination and success. Soon you'll be writing your own affirmations as you consciously create your day. Pass your own personal affirmations on to your friends and children and become an ambassador of light. You'll soon develop a practical philosophy to live by.

Carry this little book into your next staff meeting, keep it in your purse, or park it on a kitchen shelf – take it wherever your efforts are spent in changing the world. No matter where we spend time, we can thwart negativity and instead discover wonderful and unique opportunities for personal growth. If a barrage of negative thoughts enter your mind, make a commitment to arresting them! Remember, positive change in your life *always* begins with you.

Some of my ideas will give you a chuckle and, at the same time, resonate deeply with you. Whatever you've been through, I can honestly say I've been there too. By baring my soul, I hope I can help you catch negative thoughts early enough, and help you transform everyday problems into moments of potential.

I hope *The Women's Book of Empowerment* will become a friend helping you to create positive change. Remember, wisdom resides in the challenges you experience: grief, loss, loneliness, losing your job, or difficult relationships. Challenges are meant to show you what you need to learn and overcome in order to realize your own power to renovate your environment into one filled with love. Our evolution as human beings depends upon that power. You are a beautiful soul, no longer awaiting your own transformation when you choose to take charge of your thinking.

Goddess Blessings,
Charlene M. Proctor, PhD

Visit Us at www.thegoddessnetwork.net

Inspire yourself and others through positive thinking with these affirmations, posted at www.thegoddessnetwork.net. You can e-mail these lovely greeting cards to your family and friends, even to yourself, when you need encouragement. The Goddess Network is dedicated to helping women manage their multiple lives through greater self-awareness. Our job is to empower *you*. Join one of our electronic groups and send a positive thought to someone, or discuss the self-help exercises in the *Let Your Goddess Grow!* forum. Take us to Grandma's house electronically with your laptop and wireless card – there's no reason to be without support! If you have a story to share, or a new affirmation that will help other women get through their day, please register and leave your suggestion. In this way, we can become something better together by helping one another on our spiritual journeys.

WE GAIN INSIGHT BY
ALLOWING CHANGE IN
OUR LIVES AND LETTING
GO OF THE PAST.

Insight

Affirmations to gain
insight about the past

Emotions

Old negative thought patterns hold you prisoner, preventing you from moving forward into a positive state of mind and heart. They are often the most difficult to release. Our emotions are sometimes a barometer of our past. What we feel inside not only affects our entire outlook on life but makes us more susceptible to another's negativity. An affirmation encourages you to look inward to find out which elements of life are blocking your ability to mend. Change your outlook into a new assumption for today!

BOREDOM

Each day is an opportunity to stretch the limits of my mind and give more to humanity. The unlimited universe now gives me room to grow in unlimited fashion. It is time for me to step outside my space and expand my world. I give to the world with excitement and love. I have extra energy to find ways to channel my capabilities, through either this situation or another, and I am grateful that I have time to take mental, emotional, and spiritual inventory in order to improve myself and my attitude. New opportunities are coming to me now!

Burnout

My candle has been burning at both ends. Today I take the time to put out the flames and solidify. I can do one thing that makes me feel rejuvenated, and I choose not to worry about the future. By taking a moment to rekindle my flame, I grow stronger and gain perspective. New ideas refresh me in my rekindling process.

DISCOURAGEMENT

I become stronger because of the challenges I face. I am thankful for the opportunity to show others how to rise above everyday problems. Each moment I am focused by spirit to do the work I was meant to do. My heart is full with the love and support of others who help me overcome.

EMPTINESS

Today I change the way I internalize life. I inhale living spirit with every breath I take and focus my energy to help others on their soul journey. I no longer need to hold back from success and prosperity. I do not lack anything and have all the tools I need to create health, wealth, love, and happiness. I am full of my wonderful and beautiful self.

Fear

I release all fear from my physical body. I am unafraid of the future because I am part of a divine plan to cultivate my self-development. Any change in my life is met with grace and dignity. I welcome the opportunity to show others how to navigate through difficult situations without losing hope. My natural state of being is love, not fear. I reset my mental and emotional perimeter to surround this situation with divine love. I rely upon a higher power to make me stronger. It is impossible for me to attract negativity because only love can permeate my surround. Today I exist in a spiritual womb that nurtures and protects me.

FEELING LIKE A ROBOT

Today I choose to do one thing for myself that provides color in my life. I am a magnet for beauty, music, and things that smell good. I am a living, thriving human being and my senses are magnificent because they allow me to experience the world. My presence on this planet is a vital part of an intricate quilt sewn by others around me. I rejoice in my individuality!

FEELING TAKEN ADVANTAGE OF

Although I scoop up my hurtful feelings with wide arms and acknowledge them, I also release my pain. I stop allowing others to drain my vitality. I am no longer a sieve. I choose to retain my goodness and share it with others who appreciate and recognize my special talents.

FEELING UNAPPRECIATED

I know I must feel whole in order to survive life, but I cannot expect others to make me feel whole. I am already a full-fledged, complete individual with a loving heart who is empowered by purpose. What I am here to do on earth is far more important than what others think of me. I love my entire self and trust that, in the larger scheme of life, someone is thankful for what I do.

Feeling Unfulfilled

My expectations are out of alignment with what I am receiving from this situation. I release my old, negative ideas and begin filling myself with new energy and ideas. I visualize filling this gap with a combination of my energy and the energy of others. I create a new destiny for this situation by accepting energy from unknown places. I rely upon my unlimited source to fill every cell of my body with joy. I am full, robust, and renewed. From this day forward, I trust the universe to help me be more perceptive. I see signs pointing me toward activities that have my rhythm. I joyfully walk toward new adventures in life and claim them as my own.

INADEQUACY

At this moment, I am focused on my goals and not those of others. I am a piece of a universal puzzle that includes experiences and people outside my immediate realm; therefore I fit within a much larger scheme. I am filled with talent and amazing potential that is already pieced together. I love the journey I am on in life and construct my puzzle at my own pace.

LIFE PASSING ME BY

I live in the present moment; therefore it is impossible to watch the past or the future. I am fully engaged in a present life experience. I am the center of experience; I watch nothing and experience everything. My presence on earth contributes to a beautiful mosaic of everyone. I leap into life with vigor and say yes to all life has to offer!

LONELINESS

I know that reaching out to others comes back to me tenfold. Therefore, I get out of bed, get dressed, and join humanity in any way possible. Every word I speak to others, no matter how small, manifests in bigger ways. I am already creating the presence of more people in my life by my own positive and loving actions. I choose to find one living thing today to hold. As I hold a flower or a puppy or hug someone, I know I participate in the process of giving and receiving love which fills my soul. I am part of a living divine equation, and my emptiness is only a temporary illusion. I recognize, at a soul level, those who are already giving me love.

LOSING PATIENCE

The blockages I am currently experiencing are only temporary. My soul journey is unfolding at exactly the pace at which it was meant to. I trust that recent events are meant for my own self-development, and I have no need to accept punishment in any way. I do not view my situation within the confines of my own time clock. I am on the eternal time clock of the universe.

NO ONE LOVES ME

I am filled with an unlimited, inexhaustible supply of divine love. There is no greater love than the love that created my soul. My divine creator fills me with power. I am comfortable knowing that I am loved for who I am because I am a unique expression of creation. I am in love with my true self.

NOT BEING HEARD

My voice carries the energy and power of the Divine. My words are an integrated dance. As I seek others to hear my message, I rely upon my spiritual music to carry me when I no longer know how to move. My voice enhances the dance of life. I love expressing my essence because the world needs me. My voice is strong and worthy, and it is heard by those who meet me at my spiritual level. What I say is important and I lovingly express my ideas with conviction and graciousness. I am content knowing I am always heard by Mother and Father God at any moment, any place.

NOT GETTING WHAT I WANT

Today I reset my goals and priorities to a different channel. I have the power to manifest anything in my life as long as it is in tune with my higher self. I trust that my source has a higher vision for me than I could ever know. Therefore I surrender to the flow of life and allow my essence to meet an already beautiful vision of me. I am ready to receive all my good.

OVERLOOKED

I am filled with the beauty and wonder of creation. I am a flower growing in the garden of life. Other flowers do not block my sun; they provide temporary shade so I can become stronger. My presence provides diversity, which is vital to the growth of the system. I am a talented and magnificent soul!

Putting My Own Needs Last

I commit to doing at least one thing for myself today. I generate more power when I give to myself. Goodness in my life is well deserved because I am worthy of all goodness. The universe is showing me that my first responsibility is to take care of myself. When I do that, I have a bigger capacity to love others.

SACRIFICE

There can be no lack in my life because abundance is everywhere. Since there is enough for everyone on this planet, I do not have to give anything up to make room for goodness in my life. Instead I ask for divine love to help heal my situation and help me flow with the abundance of the universe instead of against it. My choices are a result of a strong will and a heart full of love. I continue to have everything I need to resolve this situation.

SELF-PITY

There is absolutely no time in life for self-pity. Retreating into self-pity disturbs my energy output and reduces my power to change the world. I am no longer battered by life. I step up to the plate with a big, powerful baseball bat and get ready to swing. I look forward to handling whatever life throws at me with vigor and ease, knowing that every day I fully engage in life I hit a spiritual home run.

Overcoming the Past

Never allow the past to hold you back from enjoying a full life. What have you got to lose, except a heavy burden? Forgiveness is usually the key to moving forward, which is why it's on the path to gaining insight. When you forgive yourself, and those who have hurt you, you are able to release negative patterns that visit you over and over again. More important, you will finally sever the control that a memory of another person has over you. Stay in the present, affirm the good that has been a result of a bad situation, and love your authentic self even more than you did yesterday. You can do it!

BAD ATTITUDE

Today I change my focus by championing a new cause. I am the ambassador of positive thinking. I spread health, wealth, love, and happiness wherever I go. I love watching how my positive statements dissolve negativity in others. I am my own instrument of renewal of positive energy, and my positive outlook is stored deep within me. Every positive statement I make is rewarded.

Can't Release the Past

Today I take all my unhappy memories out of my body and place them in a basket. My pain, my anger, and my resentments are placed in this basket. I have an angel that takes this basket of unhappiness from my hands and flies to the outer reaches of the universe and transforms it into loving energy that will revisit me later today. I forgive those around me and ask for divine assistance to hold me in a state of continual forgiveness.

FAMILY DID NOT ALLOW
ME TO BLOOM

Spring is guaranteed to come. I can bloom no matter what the weather, because I am growing spiritually each day. Today I take time to notice how I have bloomed so beautifully despite my circumstances. I am capable of reaching for the sun and sky because that is my natural state. I am reaching upward every day and do so joyfully, knowing I am grounded in the life cycle of spiritual development.

FAMILY FEUDS

I choose to be a spectator, not a participant, in negative energy generation. I facilitate healing by taking time to ask for divine assistance for this family's difficulties. I visualize these family members embracing one another for their diversity and know that each one helps another on their soul journey. Every loving and positive word I speak about my family helps to generate more healing.

FORGIVENESS

I forgive because I am capable of expressing compassion. By forgiving, I release this situation from my energy field and feel clear-headed and full-hearted. I forgive because I am able to rise to my higher self and feel lighter. My light knows no boundaries when I forgive. Life feels lighter when I forgive.

Patriarchal Attitudes in the Family

I am a spark of the Divine; therefore I am of the same soul substance as everyone else. From this day forward, I recognize my gifts of both male and female energy and reclaim a balanced image of my infinite power. Those who do not believe in me are denying part of their own divine nature; therefore they have no power over me. I am supported by Mother God!

REGRETS

Life is a curvaceous and fluid journey. Because I am always moving though learning stages, I cannot look back or measure. I learn through my relationships because that is how I begin to define who I am. Nothing is unforgivable in life. I know nursing this hurt is holding me back from fully being with others; therefore I choose to thank the universe for giving me another opportunity to develop my soul by knowing another person. I move easily through this experience.

REPEATING SAME PATTERNS

I keep experiencing the same events in my life because I have not learned a lesson at the deep level of the soul. I am committed to changing my behavior, attitude, and negative belief systems. I learn from past mistakes. Life is a self-educational process and I am a perceptive individual. I watch others as they model what I need to learn. I love all my talents as well as my imperfections because that is what makes me the beloved person I am.

Stepping Up to the Plate

We are here to learn and are not going to do everything right the first time! Quit bashing your head against the wall and know you are supported by more people than you can imagine. Do you know how many have been in your shoes? Probably thousands of people at this moment and hundreds of thousands over the course of time. You are not alone in your humanity. We're supposed to make different choices – some just turn out better than others. If we didn't have that option, there would probably be no point in being here.

FACING THE FIRING SQUAD

I am human and am entitled to goof every now and then. I choose to be humble and accept the consequences of my actions. I consider this a learning experience that makes me stronger and more compassionate to others in similar circumstances. From this day forward, my wisdom grows larger because I have had the courage to explore life in the best way I know how.

MAKING A BIG MISTAKE

I am human and I make mistakes. My self-development is enhanced when I make mistakes; therefore my error is an opportunity to flourish and grow. I am a better individual today because I accept the learning that has come from making mistakes. I celebrate my humanity!

WORRYING

I am safe and secure knowing my needs are anticipated by divine order. Today I surrender to the flow of the universe with trust. Everything I need appears at the right time. I no longer feel compelled to plan every move. I make my choices freely and look forward to the surprises that come my way, knowing they are for my higher good.

OUR LIVES ARE A
COMPLEX ROTATION OF
CIRCUMSTANCES THAT
CAN BE BALANCED WITH
OUR OWN AWARENESS AND
OUR DESIRE TO NURTURE
OURSELVES.

Balance

Affirmations that help
manage the daily complexity
of work, family, and you

Birth, Children, and Child Care

Issues surrounding children are among the most stressful we can encounter. Children test the limits of our patience. Years ago, my cousin Molly gave me a wonderful saying that has helped me keep perspective in the raising of my two sons: "Long days...short years." It's a philosophy that just about sums it up when a day with children hasn't gone so well. They're growing so fast, it'll only be a minute until they walk out the door to enter the world. Be thankful for all their stages and keep a sense of humor. That, most assuredly, you are going to need!

ADOLESCENCE

As my child transforms into an adult, I bless their growth process no matter how awkward and hurtful that might be to me. I surround their mouth with purple light and ask silently that they speak their highest spiritual truth. My well of patience runs deep. I am capable of helping this soul grow in ways that serve their higher good. There are no boundaries to my thankfulness, as I am glad to be here to guide them through these difficult years. I am capable of loving this child, no matter what they say!

Adolescent Underachiever

Today I ask the Divine to show me how I can inspire my child to step into a greater vision of who they are. I am competent enough to motivate this young soul to see the big picture. I am a vehicle of inspiration and realign my mindset to better understand where my child currently is in their self-development. I am hopeful, confident, and believe they have great potential!

BAD GRADES

My child is a genius. I believe in their talents and recognize they came here to do a specific job to contribute to the world. I ask the Divine to assist me in helping my child discover their own genius. I am a light that helps others embrace their talents and find their passion!

CRYING BABY

Today I rediscover my spiritual center, breathe, and draw strength from the Divine. I visualize an angelic and loving light surrounding my baby that is all-comforting. I am capable of seeing past today and know this is a temporary circumstance. I ask the Divine to send me someone to give me a reprieve. My energy regenerates in a way that comforts me.

FINDING A CAREGIVER

I have room in my life for a loving person who helps me accomplish my work in the world. My space has a unique and beautiful vibration that reflects the desires and needs of my family. I visualize someone moving into that space in harmony with our rhythm. I trust the universe to send the right person my way.

GRADUATION

Today I spend my time in a state of thankfulness knowing I have successfully guided this young soul to the next stage in life. This graduation is a celebration and takes nothing away from me. I release my child to the world in a state of gratitude and love, knowing their soul work is needed in the world.

MISCARRIAGE

This soul is unable to fulfill its chart at this moment. I know I have already played an instrumental part in this soul's symphony, even though I may not hear the music. I give thanks today for being a part of a perfect composition. I bless this child with love and know the choices they make are to their benefit.

Naming the New Baby

I am the life support for this soul; therefore I already resonate with this child's wants and needs. I intuitively know what this child responds to. A name carries a vibration, and I can welcome this child to their path with their own music. I am not bound by any rules. My heart knows my child's name. I am impervious to what other people think and say.

NEW BABY

I welcome this soul with all my heart! Today I celebrate the sheer wonder of new life. I am thankful for being reminded of everyday miracles. I am holding the feeling of miraculous, precious life and know this soul brings remarkable goodness to our family.

PREGNANCY

I have been blessed with the task of bringing a new soul into the world. This soul chose me for a reason and knows it can fulfill its learning journey in this current situation. I thank this child for choosing me and reassure this new life that I am here to provide them with loving opportunities to grow spiritually. I give thanks to Mother and Father God today for showing me how unlimited love can be. I feel blessed to be a co-creator of new life! Today I exist in a state of gratitude for having an opportunity to express the miracle of life. Every curve of my body expresses my female power. I love being a powerful female!

READY TO GIVE BIRTH

I am ripe with life and plentiful with the power of the Great Goddess. As I prepare to bring this soul into the world, I ask this child to always be receptive to life's wisdom. My body is beautiful. I am an abundant expression of life. I am relaxed and at ease, knowing I am a part of a vast nature cycle. I look forward to this experience and rejoice in my body's ability to regenerate life!

SICK CHILD

My ability to be kind and caring knows no boundaries. I am a nurturer of all life. My well is deep and I bring forth an unlimited source of healing energy, which is enhanced by divine love. I can channel healing through my hands, my words, and my actions. I am comforted by knowing that my child is protected and loved by a higher power.

Too Much Advice on New Baby

I love my child and am comfortable in my own beautiful space with my baby. I feel solid in my parental knowingness. I am surrounded by a window and unwanted advice falls against me like hard rain but effortlessly slides away. I feel washed clean but take away nothing unless I choose. I am competent and unfazed by others who tell me what to do.

Entertaining

Whether we love it or not, everyone knows how stressful entertaining can be, when compounded with already full schedules. Could those of you who just breeze through entertaining please tell the rest of us what affirmations you use when people don't bother to RSVP?

STRESS OF ENTERTAINING

I am totally at ease and comfortable inviting people into my energy sphere. My home and my hospitality are a demonstration of who I am, and I have nothing to prove or hide. All my anxiety and worry are dissipating as I look forward to welcoming people into a part of my world. I am a gift to those around me!

UNGRATEFUL GUESTS

The gift of my true self is fabulous no matter what other people do or say. I release all negative energy from my body and home by taking a deep breath and blowing all criticism and boorishness out the door. I no longer need anyone in my life who does not appreciate me. These people fade away toward the horizon! I release this experience and am now wiser and more in tune with my own needs.

Everyday Stress

I'm convinced we choose to attract a great deal of every-day stress on our own. I also think we program a certain amount of it in our charts before we get here. No matter what point in history we arrive at, it seems that the same everyday stress comes and goes. Where the pioneers walked ten miles to get to the store, and probably worried that there would be nothing on the shelves when they arrived, we agonize over the wasted time we spend in the checkout line. The difference between the pioneers and us is that they had a nice long walk to reset their thinking to the positive side of the dial. You do too: use your time well, rely upon your source, ask for more patience, and ride the bumps with good humor.

CAR BREAKDOWN

At this moment, I am in exactly in the place I should be. For once, I do not question life. I am inventorying all the good that has happened to me over the past year and am thankful for what I have. I am grateful for all the wonderful people in my life. With a good attitude, I get through this day with ease!

COMPLAINERS

I create distance between myself and others who are negative. I am not solely responsible for bringing their energy level higher. Although I willingly help others see the positive aspects of life, I am not responsible for their discontent. I am protected by a bubble of positive energy. My self-love keeps me positive!

LAST TO GET EVERYTHING

I am worthy to receive anything I desire. I now release old and useless patterns of thinking that make me feel unworthy. I am worthwhile and perfectly created by the Divine. I put myself at the top of everyone's list because I love myself, I love my self-worth, and I love my self-importance!

PEOPLE WHO TAKE ADVANTAGE

Today I learn to say no in a loving manner. I have the power of choice and choose to preserve my energy. I redirect my energy in ways that benefit those in need. I rely upon divine order to advise me on who I can rescue. Taking care of myself first always allows me to bring more light to others.

STUCK IN COMMUTER TRAFFIC

At this moment, I visualize a realm where I am not confined by space and time. In my mind, I am instantly there. Because I am already at my destination in my mind's eye, my body catches up as soon as humanly possible. I breathe deeply and ride the bumps in life with good humor and patience.

TRAVELING TOO MUCH

Each step in my professional world is vital to my personal goals. Divine guidance provides me with the sustenance I need to keep moving forward. Every day I appreciate the simple things that matter. By having this experience, I am more empathetic with all people in all walks of life. I thank the universe in advance for whatever goodness lies ahead in my path.

Unhealthy Work Environment

I have the ability to see beyond the material and know what is really important in life. In this job, I am thankful for my participation in the human element. My positive attitude brings joy to others who surround me. I create beauty by being present. I ask for divine protection in preserving my physical health and mental well-being in order to stand strong. Although I ask to be released from any situation that may cause me permanent harm, today I rejoice in my ability to perform a vital service for the good of humanity. I am strong, safe, and unharmed.

WAITING IN LINE

Waiting in this line gives me an opportunity to compliment someone. I recognize the positive contribution another person makes in the world, no matter who they are. My smile reflects my appreciation for the person next to me. From this day forward, every time I wait in a line, I use the time to thank or compliment someone and be cheerful. I love seeing my good energy returned in positive ways.

Family Stress

Our families provide us with some of the most challenging circumstances we will ever experience. Since family dynamics make us intimate with a situation, it is difficult to step away and separate the past from the present. Family histories are colorful and complicated, and it's not easy to stay focused on today when yesterday seems but a moment away. Focus on releasing the past and find joy in what others bring to the table. Remember, you are always defined by you, not by others, no matter how well they think they know you. Be centered, take a deep breath, and keep moving forward.

FINANCIALLY SUPPORTING EVERYONE IN THE FAMILY

I see my talents to provide for this family growing like a big tree with deep roots. I am nourished by an unlimited source of abundance. It's not money that supplies me; my awareness of the Divine within me is my constant supply. I can manifest good for those I love by letting go and trusting divine love to appear in my life and affairs.

IMPRISONED FAMILY MEMBER

This soul has charted their path according to their specifications. Although I can love them through it, they have chosen this experience for their own learning agenda. I am thankful I have an opportunity to test my strength and capacity to love another no matter what the circumstances. I have an unlimited source of love and forgiveness that grows more robust every day.

MEN HAVING POWER, WOMEN WITHOUT POWER

I have allowed others to claim power over me through faulty thinking and beliefs. I am a whole person who is cherished and loved by a power greater than what anyone can imagine. My true power is shared with Mother and Father God, who fill my heart each day. From this day forward, I speak my mind and facilitate loving action from my heart. No person can take my true self away from me.

Mentally Challenged Family Member

In this lifetime, we are all caretakers of the human spirit. Therefore this is an opportunity for our family to extend kindness and compassion beyond what we thought possible. We are an awareness channel for this person's needs. I visualize help arriving in many different directions in a balanced way. I am open to receiving loving assistance from everyone.

Negative Family Members

Each day I wake with a desire to improve. I have room for only a positive vision of what we can do with the world. Therefore I mentally put on a protective suit that no negativity can permeate. I do not alter the vision of what I can do with my life for the good of others. Negative comments flow off me like water off a duck's back. I am safe and secure in my protective, positive suit of light!

ROCK OF THE FAMILY

Others depend upon me for my deep well of strength and wisdom. I am grounded and centered. I channel spirit in everything I am asked to do. My patience is infinite because I am an extension of infinite spirit. I am thankful I can help others through their soul journey.

Ungrateful Family

Even though I do not receive thanks from those I have helped, I am stronger knowing that I can survive this situation without bitterness. Today I find ways to appreciate myself for being generous to an ungrateful family. I continue to give with a happy heart in those areas that complete my life's mission. I am free from resentment because my true thanks are manifested in other ways that are not readily seen.

WANTING A PERFECT FAMILY

I love and accept my family exactly as they are in their self-development scheme. Divine order is present in my world no matter how it may look. From this day forward, I stop focusing on what I think I lack in my family and concentrate on what I need to learn from others in my inner circle. I am in a learning environment that is already perfect for my own soul journey.

WANTING TO TRADE IN FAMILY

I chose this family when I wrote my chart for this life; therefore I am committed to seeing this experience through. I ask my higher self to show me what lessons I must learn in order to evolve my soul. Every day I develop more fortitude to endure by taking time to remember myself within the big picture. I am here for a reason and I accept these people as part of my learning experience.

Fun and Games

Life is supposed to be an adventure. Growing up, were you told that if you were playing, you were not working hard enough or being irresponsible? If you had fun, did your parents appear to feel worse because it seemed to reinforce that there was no fun in their own life? Because of past programming, we sometimes take all the fun out of having fun without even knowing why. As children, we're meant to be seen *and* heard – in great big, noisy, silly globs. Take a gulp of fun every now and then, be a kid, and forget about what you've been told in the past. At any age, our bodies need all those endorphins that laughter, exercise, and goofing around provide.

Can't Be a Kid Again

It feels great to play and relax with my children. I love to be a kid. Laughing together shows we are all worthy of having fun in our lives. I take time to play and love the child in me. Everyone in this family deserves to have fun, including me!

Can't Spend Money on Having Fun

I do not recognize any lack in the universe. My source works through me to provide what I want. I am worthy of joy and pleasure! Denying myself pleasure does not create more room for other good things to happen. There is an unlimited supply of pleasure in the universe. I now allow my income to move through me to enjoy life more fully. The channel is open between my money and accepting good, fun, and joy.

DON'T KNOW HOW TO PLAY

Today I am a playful soul-child. I look at everything with wonder and a sense of surprise. Time slows down today and each moment is a gift. I love simply being me, being free, and making it up as I go along. I have a skip in my step and stretch my arms wide to the sky to accept an unlimited universe filled with joy. I have a joyful, playful, and young spirit!

WORRIED ABOUT THE COST OF HAVING FUN

I am an image of wealth because I am my unlimited God-self. I open a clear channel to replenish my supply. Since my needs are met even before I anticipate them, I can spend money on having fun. There is no need to deny myself anything. I am an expression of wealth and abundance. There is no lack in the infinite mind of God.

Home Life

When we add up all the responsibilities surrounding our abodes, sometimes managing home life seems like orchestrating the Normandy invasion. Houses and apartments take on a life of their own and become part of the family, complete with spirit-sprites, broken dishwashers, and leaks that spring when spring has sprung. If you choose to add that element of complexity in your life, then flow with the universe instead of against it. Bless your Tara, be thankful for where you hang your hat, and know that tomorrow is another day.

Appliance Breakdown

I love my appliance and hold a positive vision of it in good health! I ask the universe to send me someone to fix this problem. At this moment, I believe it is already done and I can relax, knowing help is on the way. I thank God for reminding me that there is no point in worrying about food, laundry, or dinner because, sooner or later, it eventually gets done!

BUILDING A HOME

I can manifest anything I want in life because of my creative passion and intentions. This home is already built because I hold an image of it in my mind and see it completed. This project moves with ease and reminds me of the power we all have to manifest good in life, no matter where!

Buying a Home

I trust the universe to lead me to the right place to live. I visualize being happy and in tune with my surroundings. I am a person who lives in harmony with people and places; therefore I am already attracting the best place for myself to hang my hat!

Doing Too Much Around the House

Today I bring my awareness back into balance with my surroundings. I adjust my focus to include a healthy balance between doing and being. From this day forward, I slow down and do not try to beat the clock to create more time. I take time out of each day to recognize who I am and put a healthy portion of energy into myself as well as my home!

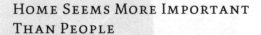

HOME SEEMS MORE IMPORTANT THAN PEOPLE

I am blessed to have people in my life who help me articulate who I am. I express myself through my surroundings and material things. My expression is what is important and not the physical objects. My home is a harmonious haven for the people I love in my life, but it can never replace anyone. From this day forward, I balance my priorities and generate a loving expression with fewer things and more joyful energy.

LACK OF PEACE AND REFUGE

I choose to keep my mindset peaceful because peace is what is demonstrated in my outer world. When my inner house is in order, I am centered and feel complete no matter where I am. I bring my inner peace to my outer world every day and convey a peaceful mindset in everything I do. I am a steady and strong peace equation. I emanate a peaceful vibration from every fiber of my being.

LEMON HOUSE

My home is filled with little spirit-sprites that are not welcome. Today I surround my home with a bright light and order them off to wherever they need to go. I ask for positive energy to fill this home. Only those energies that are for my highest good may remain.

Mundane Chores

With every household task, I practice spiritual mindfulness. I am grateful for this chore because it allows me to stabilize my mind. Although my body is on automatic pilot, I redirect my energy by going within and use this opportunity to connect with a higher power. Each task becomes a dedication to my source. I rejoice in taking care of my place in the world.

Partner Won't Help with Chores

I accept help easily in life. As I ask for help, it easily manifests in my world. I am worthy of being helped when I ask in a positive way. I open my heart and ask lovingly with good intentions. I am a magnet for action on household chores and attract household help easily by expressing my needs well.

SELLING THE HOUSE OR APARTMENT

I love my home and visualize this home making another person happy. My home is filled with positive energy and is already noticed by every potential buyer. I let this home go and become an open and perceptive buyer channel. I trust the universe to bring an offer at the right time!

SURVIVING THE REMODELING

Today I find my spiritual center within chaos. Instead of cleaning this place one more time, I take a moment to love life with all my heart. I love the earth, I love my family, and I love this mess. I am thankful for all I have. I visualize my project completed!

TRAPPED IN HOME LIFE

I am connected to the larger human and spiritual community by my thoughts, wishes, feelings, and prayers; therefore I am never limited by these four walls. My higher self is guiding me to places and prospects that are part of my consciousness. New opportunities are already manifesting in my experience. I am an open window to a beautiful world, both inside and outside my home!

Pets

My father-in-law used to spend a lot of time making jokes about the family dogs. He'd say that when he got to the other side of existence, he'd like to be reincarnated as a dog in the Proctor house. We've always laughed about the presidential treatment our pets have received – even our goldfish gets positive strokes for staying in the tank. Most of us learn to love our pets as much as people. After all, pets love you forever and are *always* interested in what you have to say.

Lost Dogs, Cats, and Other Creatures

I place a protective, loving light shield around my treasured pet for protection and ask the Divine for a safe journey home. I visualize my pet safe and happy. When I think of my pet, I am filled with comfort, which replaces any worry or pain. I trust my pet is exactly in the place it should be.

PUTTING A PET DOWN

My pet knows I am responsible for choosing the quality of its life. My love for this animal extends beyond any physical boundaries because love is forever. Therefore, my pet and I exist forever. I trust we will be together on the other side someday, and that this parting is only temporary. I release this animal to the caretakers of its spirit and trust that it is in a wonderful and peaceful place.

Vacations

You'd think taking a vacation to relax would be a logical escape from daily complexity. It turns out that going on a vacation can be at the top of the list of stresses. As spouses, parents, and partners, by the time we've met everyone's vacation needs, little downtime remains to rest our minds and get away from excessive stimuli. We also feel compelled to pack paradise into a week, so we hurry to keep up with the herd. With the bad happenings that can occur on a vacation, we need to be even more skilled at staying in the present. Expect the best, play with abandon, and affirm that the world can go on without you for a few days. Don't forget to reserve time for yourself!

BAD SERVICE

People receive exactly what they expect. I expect good service and am a magnet for positive energy wherever I travel. Only positive people who love to give good service come my way. I constantly exude an aura of thankful energy, thanking people silently for their good service before I even experience it. My needs are always met completely.

BAD WEATHER

Every element of weather is a beautiful expression of Mother God. I am in tune with nature no matter what color the sky. Today I choose to broaden my perspective and appreciate life when things don't go as planned. I use this time to renew myself, as the rain renews flowers. Every day is a blessing and an opportunity to improve the world with cheer.

Can't Mentally Go on Vacation

I am now in a peaceful place where there is no need for control. I release my worry. Relaxing gives me more physical and mental strength to channel good energy into my business when I return; therefore I completely leave all worrisome thoughts behind. My business continues to grow while I am away.

CAN'T SEEM TO GET AWAY

I make space in my life for relaxation and enjoyment. I am the master of my own routine and my own mindset; therefore I am not limited by what people say and think. I am willing to let go and trust that my needs will be met. I am safe, secure, and unafraid of new adventures. I love having new places to go!

CROWDS

This sea of humanity shows me I am part of a world equation that is more valuable than I thought. Every person I see in front of me is a loving expression of the Divine. I am irreplaceable and have an essential purpose in the world, no matter how many people I see. Each soul on this planet is a rare and tender expression of divine love.

DELAYS IN TRAVEL

The universe wants me to slow down. As I wait, I take mental inventory of what is in my mind and make sure I am on a good path. My priorities are in order. My traveling energy is smooth and fluid. There are no blockages in my path. I visualize arriving at my destination safely. I now practice everyday patience by adopting a slower and steadier pace. I notice everything good in life.

DESTINATION NOT WHAT I THOUGHT

This place is a reflection of my mental condition. I create in my life what I hold in my mind. This experience is good for me because it allows me to mentally clean house. I deserve to be in a beautiful place and now change my thinking to reflect the quality I deserve. Since I have declared that idea to the universe, it is held within my consciousness. Beautiful places and beautiful experiences are now manifesting in my world.

EVERYONE ELSE IS GOING ON VACATION

As long as I think I do not deserve to have fun, my circumstances will reflect it. I now release any old, negative patterns in my thinking that no longer support me. I deserve the very best that life has to offer. I love to have fun and enjoy myself! Pleasure and enjoyment are part of my life and I love to play. Playing is good and it makes me healthy and whole. I am an abundant and prosperous person who enjoys having fun!

GETTING LOST

I am protected by my angels, Mother and Father God, and all my spirit helpers who watch over me no matter where I am. I now ask for help to find my way. I am safe and breathe easier knowing that my higher self guides me. I trust the Divine to guide me. No thing and no person is ever lost in the mind of God.

GETTING SICK ON VACATION

At this moment, I am healing my body. I choose to be healthy and enjoy my abundant life. There is plenty of room for enjoyment. Each cell of my body is now healing and filled with joy. I take time for fun because I deserve to have fun. I let go of all my disease and worry and replace it with a child's joy. I am completely worthy of pleasure.

Going Home Early

I release all resentment and worry, knowing that this circumstance is happening for a reason. The universe is in perfect order and I now accept my orderly spot within it. Today I adopt an orderly and balanced outlook. There is no chaos – only complete divine order that unfolds in the right time, in a way that is meant to be.

HAUNTED HOTEL ROOMS

I ask that every energy form that is in this room be here for my higher good. I am safe and protected by the light of the Divine; therefore nothing can hurt me. I order all spirits out of this area that are not here for my highest benefit. I surround this area with the purest and most powerful divine light. I order all negative energy to be gone!

Lost Luggage

I trust that my items are exactly where they need to be. On this trip, I am a magnet for my own possessions. I treat my possessions with respect because they are a demonstration of divine energy and I am their temporary caretaker. I turn my concerns over to the universe and trust that divine order is at work in my life. Nothing is ever lost in the mind of God.

Nasty People

I readjust my energy pattern to attract people who are polite and cheerful by being polite and cheerful myself. My attitude is so full of love that I spill beautiful light from my heart wherever I go. Happy people are attracted to me because I am happiness. I silently bless each person I come in contact with and surround them with my light, knowing that at an invisible level, they take my loving presence with them. I am the captain of happiness and my ship sails brightly wherever I go.

OFFICE CALLING CONSTANTLY

Humans have existed for hundreds of thousands of years. The earth has existed for millions of years. The universe is timeless and has always existed, without beginning or without end. Since there always was work and will always be, it goes on without me for a while. I completely unplug from the daily brouhaha at the office and place my trust in everyone else and in the Divine. Complete and divine order is present in my office, within my mind, and in all areas of my life.

Weddings and Family Feuds

Your family exists for your own soul evolution. It's a bit hard to remember when crotchety Aunt Martha gives you a hard time at your wedding rehearsal dinner about why you and your fiancé asked for king-size bedsheets. Why in the world, she criticizes, would you need a king-size bed? Planning to have too much fun? Weddings and family get-togethers can bring out either the worst or the best in people. Breathe deeply, and have a Marx Brothers video on hand to watch when the evening ends. You'll go to bed with good energy and forget why you invited most of the family for dinner.

BAD FAMILY GET-TOGETHER

Even though my family members are out of sync with one another and with me, I am still capable of rising above this situation and taking away only the good. At this moment, I mentally retreat to a safe place where I am reminded that I am loved unconditionally. I visualize sweeping all negative comments and behaviors out an open door and watching them disintegrate into a bright light. I am unharmed and whole, and I ask the Divine to help people in my family reach their potential.

Canceling the Wedding

Today I take my first steps on a path leading toward "me." I am impervious to other people's opinions about my future. I am confident knowing there are adventures and love to be had that are not seen clearly today. This day will be remembered as one of strength and choice. I look forward to discovering the possibilities that life has in store for me.

Holiday Hassles

In the universal perspective, this holiday is but a blink in time. Therefore I move gracefully through these moments with ease. I offer others my heart without depleting my energy reserves. From this day forward, I focus on what is important about this holiday and not what I think others expect me to do. I am capable of using my tune-out button when a negative situation arises. I am centered, whole, and happy, and I celebrate life well.

Planning a Wedding: Difficult Mother and Mother-in-Law

This event is a reflection of my idea of a love celebration. My vision of this event is a gift to those I treasure in my life and not a vision of what others think it should be. Today I take charge of expressing this vision and channel my energies in a way that meets my needs. I am capable of lovingly saying no when needed and am free from other people's opinions. I look forward to the future with zest and vigor!

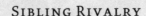

SIBLING RIVALRY

I visualize [*name of sibling*] at my side helping me conquer the darkness of the world. We are a light-team, stronger when paired. Together, we are earth workers who impart wisdom to others, especially our parents. We are one collective, positive force that can accomplish more united than apart. I appreciate [*sibling*] for joining me on my soul journey and helping me to accomplish what I set out to do.

Working Mothers

It is an undisputable fact that every mother is a working mother. Because of today's pace, mothering can be as stressful as what goes on in the office. But women who are engaged in professional environments and are also parents need even more self-discipline to stay in balance. Work stress often crosses over into a home environment, making it tricky to separate issues at the day's end. After taking care of patients or serving clients all day, how often have you reached your physical and emotional limits just by fixing tomorrow's bag lunches? And how many of you are reading the company report while spreading the mayonnaise?

Using affirmations helps you keep a balanced perspective – and stay a comfortable distance away from the edge. Balancing home and professional environments takes huge amounts of emotional and mental energy along with spiritual discipline.

Look at the big picture and feel good about what you do. The world needs you in all the glorious ways you express spirit. Arise each day with a deep feeling of trust. Someday it will all get done!

Feeling As If I'm on a Treadmill

Today I stop to smell the flowers. My life is about thinking and feeling and not all about doing. By taking care of me first, I enhance my contribution to others. I am strong enough to say no when I sense that my energies may be misdirected. I focus on choosing experiences in my life that contribute to my own spiritual development.

Guilt About Working

In my lifetime, I am meant to be a part of the larger community. Using my skillfulness is my way of demonstrating who I am. I love to express my divine gifts. I love having my presence benefit others outside my home. My family is proud that I have made a commitment to bettering the world we live in.

MISSING FAMILY WHILE AT WORK

Today I bundle my hurt into my two hands and walk to the window. I release my pain and homesickness for my family, and mentally surround them with my love. I am thankful I have an opportunity to contribute to the world, and I use my time productively. When I am home, I magnify my love for my family through loving actions.

NO TIME FOR SELF

I deserve to have time for my own interests because I am a worthy soul. Today I take time to appreciate my magnificence by not watching the clock. I rejuvenate my spirit with my feelings of self-worth. I feel more balanced and powerful when I take time for my own enjoyment. From this day forward, I no longer give any power to being an empty vessel that lacks self-worth. I am filled with life's bounty, love being alive, and love spending time with me.

Overwhelmed

Today I ask for the light of Mother and Father God to nurture me and give me strength. I allow the Divine to fill me completely with beautiful sound and color which replenishes my empty well. I arise with purpose and know I am not alone in tackling my everyday issues. Today everything I see reminds me that I am supported by a higher power.

SINGLE MOTHER DOING IT ALL

Divine order is present in each day that I exist. As I answer to the needs of my children, I know this was the path I was meant to take. I am doing a wonderful job and am growing while my children grow. I am so very thankful I have the power to choose my own path.

WE ARE EARTHBOUND IN
OUR PAINFUL EXPERIENCES,
BUT WITH THE HELP OF
OTHERS WE CAN REACH
HIGHER FOR OUR SOUL
DEVELOPMENT.

Resiliency

Affirmations to
help you become
stronger with adversity

Change

The work environment presents some of the greatest adversity we will ever experience. When our work changes, we question whether what we do for a living is our true calling, whether the world needs us, or whether working is worth the effort. Before we chuck it all to go live on a beach somewhere in our coconut bras, let's get to work with a new attitude on change. Every job leads you to higher ground. A new venue is often the most positive change you can make. Be confident and trust the universe!

ANTICIPATING UNEMPLOYMENT

Finding a new work situation requires transition and changing my old mental habits. I view this period as an opportunity to be clearer about what I want to do with my life. My hurt and uncertainty about the future leave my body before I get out of bed. Each morning I arise with an attitude of success. I believe this change is a learning experience, and I step up to this challenge with strength and conviction in what I have to offer the world.

Being Fired

I am thankful to be released from a situation that no longer allows me to grow. I am a light that has been uncovered, and now I seek to find places in the world to illuminate others with my special talents. In my new job, there are others who recognize and appreciate my potential for growth.

CHANGING JOBS

Today I commit to a new path. I am filled with excitement and anticipation of a new adventure. Those in my immediate future are already welcoming me as a positive addition to their team. Divine guidance has found the best situation for me so that my light can shine brightly.

Job Hunting

Looking for a job is an adventure. There are unlimited places for me to contribute to the world. My energy attracts the best match for my talents and capabilities. This is an opportunity to believe in what I can do. I love having the world need my skills!

MOVING ON

Today I take the first step toward new goals. I am growing by exploring new territory. Life has many lessons for me and this is only the beginning of a new, exciting adventure. With each step, I add more dimension and color to my life. Good things are happening to me now. I welcome new adventures with open arms!

Quitting a Job

I cannot continue to grow in my current work environment. I believe there are other people outside this organization who recognize my potential. I leave my current situation with grace and consideration for those who have taken me this far. I am thankful to those around me for their energy and time. New doors of opportunity are already open for me to walk through!

RELOCATING FOR CAREER

I look forward to this opportunity with hope and anticipation. My soul work takes me to another venue, where I am needed to contribute to the greater good. I am relaxed and comfortable knowing I follow a path in life that is meant to be. I move with ease and expect my life to be filled with health, wealth, love, and happiness.

TEMPORARY EMPLOYMENT

I am thankful I have this opportunity to discover my gifts. I use this time to refine my self-image. The perfect job is already available and my energy attracts a new job in an environment where positive, supportive people vibrate at the same frequency as I do. Each day is an important part of my self-discovery process.

Unemployment

Today I arise like a phoenix from the ashes. I put on a suit, look sharp, and join the rest of the world. My energy finds those who recognize my divine essence. My light is so bright; it cannot be contained by any setbacks or discouragement. I am aligned with the path that allows me to do my soul work. This experience is part of the divine order of the universe.

Death

Crossing over is a transition we don't know much about until we get there. Although we've had some wonderful people tell us about the other side, let's work on accepting life on earth for now. There's nothing to fear: we'll all be there together soon enough. Meanwhile, let's be thankful we've had these earth experiences with those we knew, loved ones or not. Everyone helps everyone evolve on their soul journey. Love lasts forever – and it will appear in many forms to help you through this life and in transitioning to the next.

DEATH IN FAMILY

No matter how painful this day, I know there is a higher power at work in my life. I surrender to the joy and pain we are meant to experience and accept these circumstances as part of my charted plan. Everyone and everything is part of a cycle of birth and renewal. Today I trust the unknown and take comfort in knowing that we all exist and are loved, no matter what side we exist on.

DEATH OF A CO-WORKER

I accept that everyone's path is charted according to their own divine plan. I surrender to the joy and pain that we are meant to experience. Everyone and everything is part of a cycle of birth and renewal. Today I feel secure trusting the unknown and am comforted by knowing that all life is eternal.

DEATH OF A PARENT

I have completed this relationship to the best of my ability and accept death as a part of the universal cycle of birth and renewal. Today I do not question the past but only exist in the present. I place my heavy heart in the arms of a loving creator. I surrender to the joy and pain I am meant to experience. From this day forward, I am free of the past and move forward in life with a more loving perspective.

DEATH OF A PATIENT

I have done my very best in preserving this person's human life force. Although I can repair the body, it is only a vehicle for the soul. I am not capable of controlling all the elements within this person's soul journey. I release this person to a loving environment of perfect health and happiness.

DEATH OF A PET

Because I trust the universal rhythm, all arrivals and departures from earth happen at the right time. When I think of my pet crossing over, I send light and love and release it from its earth life. I give silent thanks that my life has been so enriched by its presence.

GRIEF FROM LOSS

My heartache fills my entire body today, but I know the love I have for this person who has crossed over is far greater than my heartache. From this day forward, each time I feel my heart ache from the absence of this person, I will focus on the love they brought into my life. I am so very thankful to have been blessed by their presence. No one is ever lost or gone forever, because love lasts forever. Every time I feel a heartache coming on, I send out a greater amount of love to the outer reaches of the universe and beyond. I am comfortable knowing this person will receive my love, every day and through every loving thought.

Divorce

Starting over from painful circumstances is never easy, especially when we have invested so much of our energy into others. We tend to look at people as energy investments. But no matter how the energy stock may rise and fall, it is a certainty that energy is limitless and so is your capacity to love. Be comforted, believe in what you do and who you are, love your self, and move forward. The world needs you and all you have to offer!

DIFFICULT EX

Lacking what I wanted from this relationship has been a bitter pill to swallow. I take a moment to taste the bitterness of the past, and then mentally replace it with forgiveness. I release past hurts and replace them with joy. I know there is sweetness to be found in my life, in ways that are tender and nurture me. Today I make a commitment to notice all the goodness that has been a result of this relationship. I forgive this person for their inadequacies and release them to another learning situation.

Divorced Parents

I have been placed in this situation to learn how to find the middle ground in all aspects of my life. Today I compensate for imbalance by appreciating both my male and my female energies. I choose to cultivate a healthy attitude of relationships by remembering that love is always unselfish. I forgive my parents for past hurts. I release past pain forever and replace it with an image of unlimited love. With divine love at work in my life, I am never alone or abandoned.

Ex-Husband Has a New Girlfriend

I let go of the past that no longer serves my higher good. I heal at a new level where there is no room for jealousy and resentment. If I sense space inside me, it is only because I am a vessel to receive more loving circumstances from life. I no longer reject anyone else's happiness. When I resonate happiness for others, it returns to me instantly.

FACING DIVORCE

I leave this relationship with grace and dignity. I know my own soul must grow in an area outside the perimeter of this relationship. No matter how painful the past, I am thankful that this venture has been part of my learning journey because it helps me to further define myself. My ability to give and receive love remains intact. My heart is healing. I have tremendous capacity to love others, no matter what the circumstances.

LACK OF FINANCIAL SUPPORT
FROM EX

I know I am safe, and I let the past go. As I release the past, I make room for more abundance in my life. As I heal, I am surrounded by more magnetic and powerful love so prosperity can take hold. The universe provides me with everything I need. I rely upon my source for what I want and not upon other people who do not contribute positively to my life. Divine order is present in my life each day and in every way.

LOSING CHILDREN IN DIVORCE

I bless my children knowing that love knows no distance. With each step I take today, I find courage to move forward. Every day I release pain and replace it with the love that is at work in my life. I am never alone because love is permanent and with me always. Today I ask the Divine to support me in each new step I take. No matter the distance, I always help my children cultivate love in their life.

Health

Being bombarded by the media about what's required to stay healthy can be overwhelming. Every time we pick up a magazine or turn on the television, there's a qualified spokesperson telling us exactly what we need. Start by being a magnet for good health: have a positive, strong, loving image of your body, and remember that you are a contributing partner and can't expect someone to do it all for you. Have a balanced mental, physical, emotional, and spiritual formula for nourishment. Strive for clarity in your intentions in all areas of your life and love your body no matter what. You're going to get only one – no exchanges given!

ADDICTION

I no longer run from life. I now fully engage in what life has to offer. I rise above any physical need that does not contribute to my overall health and well-being. I do not need any substance to hide from life because I love what I have to offer. I am the parent and my body is the child. I take care of my child-body with love because I love my beautiful self.

CANCER

Nothing is fatal in the mind of God. Life is robust and I choose to live my live with a joyful attitude. I release all deep resentment and forgive others who may have done me harm. I release all emotional hurt, grief, and lack from my mind and body and choose to live life with vigor. I know I have a valuable place in the world because I make a difference by being here.

Chronic Fatigue

I jump into life's flow with enthusiasm. Each day is a new adventure and the world needs my contribution. I love what I have to offer the world and to other people in my life. I am being focused by spirit to do the work I was meant to do; therefore I am constantly evolving. Each day I offer the world a newer and improved version of me. I love being part of life's process!

Chronic Pain

I no longer need to feel guilty about anything. I release all my guilt and pain together. Releasing all pain allows me to move forward in life and bring the world my true self. I visualize my heart with wings as I fly upward from my body into a blue sky. My wings release the past and fan it away forever. I love being free and deserve all goodness that comes my way.

CONSTANT SICKNESS

I am safe and protected. There is a higher power at work in my life with each step I take in the world; therefore I am unafraid of life. I have a healthy body and appreciate every detail of my human system. My body consists of vital energy that flows vigorously at every moment, and any disease is washed away. I am renewed and full of vitality. I am balanced and unafraid.

DEPRESSION

I am not limited by any person or any circumstance. I rise above negativity on this planet and choose to live with hope. Every day brings something fresh and new into my experience. I am positive and happy, and good things are happening to me now. I am no longer afraid to accept the goodness of life. With each moment, I become more perceptive of where my goodness arrives.

EATING DISORDER

I choose to nourish my body because I am a worthy soul. My soul is a beautiful expression of the Divine, and my body houses my soul. I love to take care of my body because I am needed to express my joy in the world. I love being alive and look forward to what life has to offer. I am in love with nurturing my spiritual and physical self.

Facing Surgery

I am brave and place my trust solely in the hands of the Divine. My body is protected by a green healing light that surrounds every molecule of who I am. My mind is within this healing light as it cleanses all negative thoughts. I am now on a path toward complete health and positive thinking. From this day forward, every thought I have is accompanied by a picture of a healthy body.

MENOPAUSE

All stages of my life cycle are normal and I lovingly embrace each stage. My body is a miracle and I am in love with my body. I am unafraid of aging because it only means my energy can be directed at spreading my wisdom to others. I love this stage of my life because I have so much experience and wisdom to offer others. I have a secure and important place in the world.

Menstrual Problems

I am a beloved and sacred soul within a female body. I love my body and love being female. I am fulfilled by being female, which is a divine expression of spirit. My female power balances me in all phases of my life. I visualize rising above my pain body to a place where water runs clean, cool, and calm. I feel refreshed by this current because it restores my rhythm.

OVERWEIGHT

I am in the process of creating a beautiful and meaningful life. I am safe and protected by Mother and Father God every day. I no longer have a need to hold on to the past because today is what matters. The past has no power over me. I am grown up and step into a complete vision of myself. From this day forward, I take responsibility for my life and shed old mental habits that do not support a healthy vision. I love taking care of my beautiful body!

PLASTIC SURGERY

I am my own instrument of renewal. Each day I continue to learn and grow, which refreshes my spirit. My true self shines through every pore of my being no matter what I look like. I know my power comes from the Divine. I am a channel for love and I open my heart willingly and allow my power to flow outward.

Premenstrual Syndrome (PMS)

My body is filled with female power. I love being female because I am an amazing example of the ability of the regenerative powers of life. I carry within me a blueprint of all female capability and talent; therefore I stand tall and strong in my space in the world. I think clearly and take charge of my life.

SLEEPING TROUBLE

I trust that divine order is at work each day of my life; therefore I release all worry, resentment, and fear as I drift off to sleep. My mind is filled with a vision of a new day filled with possibilities. I turn all negative thought over to my spirit guardians and let them sort it out. When I sleep, my inner house becomes ordered and peaceful, and I am prepared for the next day. I refresh my screen trusting the universe knows what is best for me.

I SHED MY SHADOW SIDE
IN ORDER TO DISCOVER MY
AUTHENTIC SELF.

Your Authentic Self

Affirmations to help you
define who you are and
know your true self

Love and Relationships

Everyone is enrolled in Soul 101. *Objective of this course:* Perfecting the soul through life's experiences, in order to realize oneness with the All. *Prior coursework recommended but not required:* Former lives, difficult parents, disappointments, and changing expectations. Student should appear with a desire to learn. With a minor in love and relationships, you'll graduate summa cum laude, as people supply us with some of the most interesting and challenging circumstances we'll ever see. Have faith – and know that all homework eventually gets finished.

ARGUMENTS

I no longer struggle to be heard because my expressive energy already communicates who I am by simply being. My voice is powerful and words no longer matter. I rest easy knowing I can speak my highest spiritual truth. My true power comes from within on the wings of divine spirit and is not defined by anyone else.

BIG-SPENDER SPOUSE

I choose to take action to remediate this situation. Today I willingly share my energy to bring this individual self-awareness in the best way I know possible. In life, we must often be loving educators for others. This lesson stretches the limits of my capabilities, and I step up to my challenge the best way I know how. I trust the spirit within to lead me.

BUM MAGNET

I am worthy of love in every aspect of my life because I am a beloved individual. I deserve all goodness that comes my way. I am empowered knowing I am divine substance; therefore, I can attract only those who recognize my own divinity. I am no longer needy because I do not recognize any lack in my life. I am full of my true self and feel whole. I am composed of pure divine love.

Can't Find a Relationship

My path to love is no longer littered with rocks and diversions. I sweep away each disappointment with ease. At this moment, I am becoming more open-minded and loving to everyone around me. From this day forward, I rejoice in my learning journey and put my love path to music. I am an incredible soul who can dance on any path.

CHEATING PARTNER

Although I have questioned my own self-worth, I now shed any doubts I have about my worthiness. I rise today standing tall and proud of who I am. No matter what the circumstances, no person is capable of diminishing my divine substance. Despite past hurt, my heart is filled with the power of spirit. I ask for divine guidance to help heal my hurt and allow my heart to overflow with love once again. I am worthy of love and now open myself to receiving love from every area of my life.

DOMINEERING PARTNER

My perception of power in this relationship is balanced by
changing my attitude. I am a spark of the Divine and my soul
substance is the same as that of any other individual. I view
this relationship as an opportunity to learn how to express
my true self. Every day, and in every way, I communicate my
deepest desires out loud and manifest my dreams into reality.
My power comes from within.

Don't Feel Special

I am an important and unique spark of the Divine, just like everyone on this planet! There is but one dimension of love and we all channel from the same source. There is but one universal order, even though we may speak to that voice in different languages. I am challenged to step outside my intellectual boundaries and facilitate a loving acceptance for people in my life, no matter how they label their source. I am a universal human filled with the presence of the Divine wherever I go.

ENDING A RELATIONSHIP

Life is a process of growth and attunement to my higher self. This relationship does not allow me to grow and fulfill my destiny. I release this person with loving hands to the world where they can be of greater service. From this day forward, I plant myself in new, fragrant soil and work with life harmoniously to grow deeper, with stronger and wiser roots.

EXPECTING PARTNER TO CHANGE

Changes I want to see in others are a mirror reflection of what I need to change in my own behavior and life. I breathe easier knowing other people are showing me what I need to learn. I am thankful I have a partner to help me discover what I am capable of becoming. In a loving way, I allow this person space to develop for their greater good while observing what inner work I need to do. I am unafraid of change.

Falling in Love

Today I rejoice in the cosmic power of love. Without analysis, I surrender to passion, pain, and walking an unknown path. I break open my heart even further in order to receive more love. I leave logic behind. By knowing love, I am experiencing the highest power possible. I use my love power to manifest good in my life, no matter the outcome of this relationship.

Falling out of Love

I am allowed to change my mind and heart for my own good. I choose all relationships in my life out of strength, not necessity. I now release all guilt. I march to the beat of my own drum, knowing I can find other hearts that beat to the same rhythm as mine.

FEELING TRAPPED IN
A RELATIONSHIP

I am a confident, worthy person. By opening doors in my situation, I am allowing my light to shine out to the world. My light always overcomes any darkness I may have experienced, and I rise to the sky in a beautiful light. I leave the past behind and am happily perched above the world. The world exists in the palm of my hand as I look forward to the future.

GETTING DUMPED

The universe is showing me that this relationship is not for my benefit. Because my path has been readjusted for my own good, I accept this decision with ease. There are bigger, better, and happier circumstances already here. I trust the universal pattern. I move forward knowing I am a beautiful jewel who is always discovered by loving people.

LACK OF COMMUNICATION

While in this relationship, I first take time to heal myself. Even though I am a whole individual, I discover the parts of me needing attention and bring them into balance. I no longer feel lack when I am in balance; therefore I re-enter this relationship with a balanced sense of my true self. My wholeness eliminates the need for another to think or feel for me.

LOSING ATTRACTION FOR EACH OTHER

I revitalize this relationship by loving who I am more each day. My loving state of mind makes me a magnet for goodness in my life. I am whole, strong, and beautiful. My loving heart always attracts other people and positive situations. When I wholeheartedly love my true self, others see my sparkling light. I love my sparkling self!

LOSING IDENTITY IN A RELATIONSHIP

I am a shining star among many constellations and my light is bright and unique. I occupy space in the universe that no one else can. This relationship is very small compared with my important place in the sky. There are many who navigate by me, and I feel full knowing how my powerful light illuminates across the miles. I make a difference in millions of lives.

PARTNER DOES NOT SUPPORT MY CAREER

This situation is testing my ability and desire to express my essence. My work allows me a special environment to develop my own capabilities and more clearly define who I am. Because I am needed in the larger community, I feel glad to be alive. I stay centered knowing what I do benefits many people.

Partners Changing at Different Paces

I came to earth for the spiritual curriculum. Although I can take a class with others who think the way I do, the best learning comes in a diverse environment. I embrace change in every aspect of my life because I have a chance to observe more of what earth has to offer. I fine-tune who I am by experiencing change and seeing change in others. I am unafraid of change!

Passive Partner

I am capable of giving my partner room to bloom. Although they are responsible for their own growth, I provide a fertile, expansive environment and help them discover who they are. I am lovingly sensitive to my partner's needs and believe my presence has a positive effect as long as I feed them with gentle understanding. I enjoy helping others on their soul journey.

Power Struggle with Spouse

Today I stop resisting the flow of life and let go. I am on my own soul journey, and it is not a competition or a race. My path is the only one of its kind and I travel at my own pace. I am now accomplishing great things and am stepping into my self-vision at exactly the right time according to a universal rhythm.

RELIGIOUS DIFFERENCES

I have a direct relationship with my own image of a loving creator; therefore I am not accountable to any other spiritual rules. My own form of spirituality nurtures me and allows me to evolve. I have a choice in the form of spirituality I practice. I resonate and grow within my own spirituality.

Sex Not Good Any More

I rejoice in my body and my ability to provide pleasure. Sharing my body with another celebrates the act of all creation and is a sacred expression. Because I fully open my heart to my partner and focus on now, not the past or the future, I have no expectations. I fully surrender to a passionate energy that knows no boundaries.

SPOUSE MAKES MORE MONEY THAN I DO

My abundance flows *through* people, not *from* them. I invite wealth and opportunity to come my way through other people. I recognize that money may come to me in unexpected ways. I have a heart filled with gratitude that my supply has come to me through someone I know. I joyfully accept this demonstration of abundance in my life by thanking the universe. I thank the Divine for sending me abundance in this surprising and creative way.

TOO MANY EXPECTATIONS

Although I am an expression of light in all I do, and can enact tremendous worldwide change, I do it one step at a time. Today I breathe easier knowing I do not have to solve everyone's problems at this very moment. I am centered and grounded. I trust my own sense of priority and rely upon divine order to guide me.

Mavericks

No two artists could possibly interpret a landscape in identical fashion. Think about that from a self-development perspective. You are going to experience the world through your own eyes, and not the eyes of others, because there is an infinite number of ways to experience, and express, the range of emotions. It's a good thing we don't all paint like Mondrian. Make your impression on the world without compromising your vision, and savor the maverick in you. Dip your brush in, continue to paint your soul story – and affirm that you are always, no matter what your style, part of a loving composition.

BLACK SHEEP

Others perceive me exactly the way I perceive myself. Therefore I choose to bring out my beloved and true nature, which is composed of pure love and light. I no longer accept any stigma or negative labels that others have placed on me. I fit perfectly in a space that has been designed exclusively for me. I love my unique space. I fit beautifully into this world and am of value to everyone in this family.

Choosing a Different Life Than Parents

I march to the beat of my own drum with a glorious rhythm. My music stems from expressing who I am in my work, play, and relationships. I am free from any expectations others have placed on me because I choose to live freely. My presence provides a learning environment for my family, just as my family's presence also helps me on my soul journey.

In-Laws Don't Like Me

Today I bundle my hurt from being unaccepted by others and release it into a bluebird-blue sky. From this day forward, a blue sky reminds me of how special I am and of my inherent freedom to spread my beautiful light. Every day, in every way, I fly higher in my capacity to forgive. The higher I go, the more my love expands to the dimension of an unlimited sky. I am no longer restrained by anyone, anything, or any circumstance that involves judgment.

New Partner, Spouse, or In-Law

From this day forward, I choose to never compromise my beautiful soul for the sake of fitting into a program. I ask for divine assistance in bringing my light in positive ways to this family. I am a whole and complete individual and am comfortable in my uniqueness. I love myself and lovingly express who I am, knowing my presence is a gift to everyone in this family.

Ostracized by Family

I am part of a larger family called the human race; therefore I am always part of a family. I love to love others in my life who have become my family. Every day I add one more person to my family in my mind and heart. I am content knowing I am loved and appreciated by many people.

PARENTS DON'T LIKE SPOUSE

At this moment, I focus on my own choices in life. I stand beside my spouse out of love. My parents are incapable of seeing what I see in this individual; therefore I choose the present moment and live my life to the best of my ability. I release all bitterness and forgive my parents for their judgments.

PARTNER'S FRIENDS DON'T APPROVE OF ME

I answer to no one but the Divine. I need only my self-approval to continue on my light path. By cultivating good everywhere, I receive protection along the way. I am confident knowing my intentions are right, and I continue to channel my energies toward creating greater good in the world. I spend my energy pursing my self-development, not in changing others' opinions of me.

Untraditional Wives, Mothers, Women, Partners

I love myself with every fiber of my being. I have nothing to prove to anyone and I define my own success. I am a unique, beloved, and cherished individual who creates reality by dreaming big. My dreams are what raise the collective vision of everyone around me. The world needs my diversity to transform and evolve.

Parents

When a child makes a clay pot, parents have a tendency to keep adding more weight here and there, as they walk by to inspect the work. Although their intentions may be noble, at some point the pot will be thrown off balance, sometimes causing it to spin wildly out of control. Before your pot falls off the wheel, take stock of who you are and hold fast: nobody can add or take away anything without your permission. Remember, *you* hold the design of your self between your own two hands, because your true self is not what others say it should be. Bless your parents, thank them the best way you know how, and lovingly cradle your own life. You'll create beauty beyond your wildest imagination.

AGING PARENTS

My parent's life force is winding down. I can provide support where needed because my source is unlimited. I am capable of loving my parent through this final phase of their earth life. Today I am reminded that I am supported by a higher power that provides me with patience and compassion.

AMBIVALENT PARENTS

I selected my parents because I wanted space to discover who I am. I have the creative power and the good sense to use my time in constructive ways. I choose to fill this empty space with a bigger vision of what I can accomplish in this lifetime. My freedom accelerates the joy I have in knowing I can accomplish anything my heart desires.

Controlling Parents

My parents brought me into this earth world but I do not belong to them. I belong to spirit. My power comes from the Divine, who replenishes me with an unlimited supply. I control my own destiny and life-learning agenda. I am worthy and strengthened by a higher power each day. I am free from any power other than my own. I feel safe knowing I am protected by the Divine.

DIFFICULT IN-LAWS

I have a lot to offer my spouse and the world. It is impossible for me to compromise who I am for the sake of another person. I make a positive contribution by being in this family. If others do not recognize my light, it is because they choose not to see it. My light is very bright and cannot be judged, quantified, or redesigned. I no longer rely on family feedback to choose a course of action! I love my self and am worthy of love.

DIFFICULT PARENTS

I selected these parents long before I arrived on this planet in order to evolve my soul. My chart includes many people challenges. I accept my learning situation. I need to strengthen my resolve by working through difficult family situations. Today I rely on spirit to assist me in taking the high road. I am a willow branch that bends in the wind but never breaks. I am a fantastic and beautiful soul!

PARENTING A PARENT AS AN EMOTIONAL CRUTCH

Today I am free from feeling responsible for another's happiness and well-being. My parent has a responsibility to stand up and choose their own course of action. I am released from burdensome and impossible expectations. I claim my life as my own today and rejoice in my emotional strength to say yes to independence!

PARENTING A PARENT FOR HEALTH REASONS

When I am the parent, I choose to be loving and generous. This is an opportunity to show how I can bring spirit into a difficult situation. I play this role without losing a sense of who I am. I am capable of compassion, which brings out the best in me. I offer compassion and healing to this situation through my hands, through my heart, and in every word I speak. God's perfection is reflected in me.

Parents Who Favor Other Children

My life is governed by choice, intention, and the guidance of the Divine, and not by what others think of me. Like everyone on this planet, I am loved equally and unconditionally by the Divine. Since I am already completely filled with love, I have enough to give others who do not love me. My situation is showing me I have a greater capacity to love. I accept this challenge by loving all people I encounter in life.

SMOTHERING PARENTS

I fill my body with fresh air today that expands my horizons. With every breath I take, I inhale confidence to succeed. I am boosted by cosmic energy and I feel buoyant knowing I can soar as high as the clouds. I am not limited by anyone's vision of what I can do. I am filled with joy as I rise to meet my true nature, knowing my special talents contribute to the greater good.

THANKLESSNESS OF PARENTING

I give unconditional love to my children. Because I love freely and completely, I am already filled with love and thanks. I accept my responsibilities and rejoice that I am able to provide my children with the tools they need to enjoy life. I am content knowing I am doing a fabulous job. I love to give the gift of love!

UNDERACHIEVER PARENTS

My parents have believed in lack and I do not. I believe in abundance and I can manifest any situation in my life I desire. My success and worth are measured by my own belief system and not by that of my parents. I love to manifest good in my life because I am in harmony with the laws of the universe. The source is unlimited and so am I. I can achieve anything by setting the right intentions, believing in what I can do, and being thankful for my gifts.

Visiting a Difficult Parent

My parental relationships are my mirror. When I set myself free from any criticism and negative thinking that have been part of my past, I am free to create exactly what I want in any relationship and in any part of my life. I chose this family because they are helping me along my own soul journey. I give thanks for arriving in a powerful and positive place in my own mind. There is no need to revisit old mental patterns, and I hold strong when challenged. I rise above any difficult circumstances without feeling any need to revisit the past. I visualize this trip as a harmonious experience. In the present moment, I am an absolutely magnificent and powerful individual!

Self-Image

What we see in the mirror is only a fraction of who we are and doesn't include our sense of humor, courage, wisdom, or capacity to love. Remember that the next time you watch the plastic surgery channel: although looking fabulous makes us feel fabulous, keep it in perspective. Your self-image includes so much more. Wouldn't it be great if we could wear our essence as easily as a new makeover? For a free facelift, read on: it's called the charismatic smile of self-love. Wear it more often and you will spread your light, making heads turn faster than a new pair of eyebrows.

AGING

Each stage in my life is wonderful. My wisdom and experience acquired from life make me a person who has a lot to offer the world. Every moment I continue to engage in the world is valuable to others. I no longer need disease or illness to secure a place in the world. I am shining, with all my wisdom, in my security. I feel safe knowing no one can take my place.

AGING PARTNER

Life is an eternal song from the Divine. I hear the song of youth inside my partner, and I embrace each youthful memory because it is part of a composition we have created together. I choose to see the good in the past and in today. From this day forward, we are full of youth through our hearts, not our eyes.

AGING WOMAN

I am proud of my wisdom. I continue to navigate through life well and contribute in immeasurable ways. I feel confident in my journey because of what I know and stand taller today because I have earned my wisdom. My appearance is beautiful, wise, and honored by everyone I meet.

BAD HAIR DAY

Inner beauty emanates from my heart center. No matter what I look like, others see me as I truly am. I am a beautiful, courageous soul who is unafraid to let life ruffle me. Today I let my hair run wild like the wolves and I dedicate myself to the beautiful, wild, free, and fierce female spirit within all women.

BAD SELF-IMAGE

When I look in the mirror, I see a loving person. My capacity to love knows no boundaries. I accept myself and love what I see in the mirror. There are no imperfections because I am perfectly constructed. I am an example of a miracle and a spiritual work in progress.

Bad Sexual Self-Image

My sexual nature is a symbol of God's perfection and an example of the power of all creation. Every aspect of my body is a reason to rejoice in life's sensations. I feel powerful by being alive. I feel blessed to be able to express my sacred gift. I choose to share my power and my body with others who recognize my gifts.

Don't Like People

My home is humanity, and I am proud to be part of an energy that is a demonstration of divine creation. Everyone I see is a beloved part of all that exists, and no matter what I think, my heart tells me that each individual makes a unique contribution to the world. In my mind's eye, I embrace the essence of all people and silently thank them for showing me a part of who I am.

Don't Like to Exercise

My body is an extension of my mind. Just as I exercise my mind with new thoughts, I move my body to keep it alive and nourished. I am flexible in my thinking and create more flexibility in my life by moving my body. I love my body because it is a miracle. I am thankful for this beautiful body and lovingly take care of it!

DRINKING TOO MUCH

I care about life and my contribution to the greater good. Every day my loving attitude makes a difference in the world. I no longer reject myself and retreat from life. I am fully engaged in the process of discovering who I am and what I can offer to others. I am aware of my unique and special capabilities. From this day forward, I turn outward for my own benefit and the benefit of others.

EATING TOO MUCH

Today I reset my priorities to include a healthy and nourishing routine. My diet is about purging all negative thoughts, including guilt. I love and approve of my body and of myself. I shed this weight easily as I become more positive, lighter, and in love with my true self. I am not afraid of being on this earth. I am protected by Mother and Father God, who watch over me at every moment. My path is safe and I feel good about being here. I am unafraid of my emotions because they are a normal part of who I am. I love feeling safe and protected. From this day forward, I choose a healthy and nourishing diet and state of mind.

LAZINESS

I am grateful I have skills and talents that can serve humanity. Today I arise with renewed vigor, knowing I influence more people than I can possibly imagine. The entire planet is a better place because of what I offer. I now choose a new attitude about working because I believe the world needs my contribution.

Morning Blues

Today I swing my legs over the side of the bed and get up knowing my contribution to the world is important. This is an exciting time to live on earth because there is much work to be done. I join the world knowing I make a positive contribution at every moment. The world needs me to be present. I am satisfied knowing my life makes a big difference.

Shyness

Every step I take today gives me confidence in who I am. I am a treasure chest, and today I find one more person to guide my own hand to open me up. I trust myself and can learn to trust others in discovering my treasure. I spread my arms wide to the sky every day and inhale confidence with every breath I take.

UNRECOGNIZED TALENTS

I am a unique and beloved individual who has already changed the world by being present. I am filled with joy knowing I have offered the world my gifts. I shine no matter what my family says; my talents reach far outside of this realm. I now focus on what my talents can do for the greater good. I love what I can do!

I HAVE EVERYTHING I
NEED IN LIFE. MY SUPPLY
IS LIMITLESS AND I
CONTINUALLY ACCEPT
GIFTS FROM THE UNIVERSE.

Abundance

Affirmations that help you
create a mental equivalent to
manifest what you desire

Financial Attitudes and Behavior

Let's change those negative assumptions about money before you run off to the next shoe sale. You can have what your heart desires because your source makes it impossible for you to be anything but abundant. Prosperous thinking includes seeing abundance in everything in your purview – including what you offer to the world in the form of your true self. Work with universal order by knowing that you are worthy of abundance, and set your mental state on a new, steady, and prosperous course. You can demonstrate the life you want to live!

ALWAYS STRUGGLING

I live life with ease. I expand my mind to include what I desire in life. I ask, and I know I am worthy of receiving. I open my heart to a new level of thankfulness and recognize all the good in my life. I love being prosperous because it is my natural state. I go with the abundant flow of life and do not paddle against the current. My ride is joyful and easy and includes everything I desire.

Can't-Afford Mindset

When I dwell on the idea of lack, I build a consciousness of lack and it attracts more lack. Whatever I ask for, I receive, because the natural state of the unlimited universe is to provide for me. I now have a mindset of abundance because my source is unlimited! I am part of a universal order that provides an abundant and inexhaustible supply. I see abundance reflected in all areas of my life. My income and all things that are valuable to me are prospering and growing bigger as I notice how much abundance there is in the world.

CAN'T ATTRACT MONEY

Today I stop focusing on attracting money and focus on my source, which is my unlimited supply. My source is the foundation of prosperity. From this day forward, I inhale abundance and permanently bring it into my awareness. I choose to identify with my source; therefore I am abundance and prosperity. I am now aligning my higher self with a vision of prosperity. I exhale success and satisfaction with each breath.

CARELESSNESS ABOUT MONEY

I treat money with respect. I pick up every coin off the street with a heart full of thanks and take care of it lovingly until I spend it. I lovingly store my wallet and purse in a safe place, because I am the temporary caretaker of my money. My money actions place value on the idea of money and make it a valuable part of my life; therefore I treat my money valuably. When I spend or give money away, I do so happily and silently bless each person my money comes in contact with.

Cheapness Is Virtuous

I am in tune with the rhythm of life and its natural ebb and flow. I do not arrest the natural flow of the world – I recognize I am part of the flow. I give and receive with the tremendous energy of love. My energy of giving and receiving is powerful and brings more good to others and to me. I love being generous because all I release returns to me.

Complaining About Money

I am thankful for what I receive and remain open to receiving more. Each time I feel the urge to complain about money, I replace it with a thankful statement. I turn every complaint into a compliment. When others complain about money, I express thanks out loud for the good in the world. I am an ambassador of abundance energy because I transform negativity into thankfulness.

DON'T DESERVE TO BE RICH

My prosperity is a mirror of my own thoughts. Today I expand my vision of abundance by accepting my own worth. I am a worthy person and deserve the best in life. I already trust that the universe guides me in making good and beneficial choices; therefore I am unafraid of being rich. I deserve all good that comes my way. I love being in an abundant state because the universe knows no boundaries in providing as much as I want and need.

ECONOMY IS IN SHAMBLES

Because we are all spirit, we are all part of the source. Whatever I say about others, I am saying about my self. When I see others, I also see my self; therefore I choose to see everyone and everything as full and fulfilled. I see the world as robust, filled with opportunity, and richly abundant; therefore I attract those ideas into my life. Our economy is healthy and we are all part of an abundant and prosperous equation.

EVERYTHING IS TOO EXPENSIVE

I can demonstrate anything in my life that I want with the right mental mindset. If I label everything in a way that is unachievable for me, then I cannot achieve it. From this day forward, I replace my words with a vocabulary of prosperity. I can afford anything and everything because I am open to abundance in all avenues in my life. I am worthy of having things of worth.

In Love with Money

Money is not my source. My inexhaustible source is the divine presence within me. Money is an effect which has no value in itself because it is a symbol. Money is a symbol of an idea of infinite surplus to which I belong. I now focus on the cause of money, which is my awareness of my spirituality. I do not allow my money effect to have power over me. Instead, I embrace the idea that the Divine is my supply. My supply flows freely because I love my source, and not the effect.

LACK IS A CONSTANT WORRY

What I want in my life I think about. What I don't want in my life, I don't think about. From this day forward I stop thinking about lack because I don't want lack in my life! I replace those thoughts with a vision of a beautiful garden, with fruit, flowers, and vegetables growing in rich abundance. I know this garden is a reflection of my life. My garden is overflowing with supply and enriched by the abundant world we live in.

LACKING ABUNDANCE

Because the world is a perfect gift, I already have everything. I accept my gifts with joy. Every day I rise in a state of thankfulness for all that exists, especially for the blessings in my life. I exist in a state of peace and thankfulness for what I have, knowing that the universe is working with me to manifest what I desire. I do not believe in lack; I believe in prosperity, which is my natural state.

MONEY AS MOTIVATOR

My fixation on money alone has translated into lack. The universe is showing me that I cannot generate wealth unless I view money only as an intermediate step to getting what I want. I know there is an abundant supply of everything I need. From this day forward, I visualize what I desire instead of the money I think I need to get it.

MONEY IS POWER

My center, my power, my source is my God-self. I am a spark, a piece of individualized consciousness. The greater my awareness of my true self, and the more knowledge I have of my own divinity, the more I become an expansive, compassionate, loving, and powerful individual. My power is drawn from my unlimited source. I am nourished and replenished every day and in every way.

MONEY NEVER COMES EASILY

I am grateful for every gift in my life. I am an open channel to receiving all my goodness, no matter where it comes from. I am now opening the door to an abundant and prosperous world, and I step through with joy. I love being receptive to all good in my life. I thank the universe for every gift that comes my way and know I am always ready to receive my good from everywhere, everything, and everyone.

Not Meant to Have Money

I love my true self. I am a worthy, deserving, and beloved individual. I am not limited by anything or anyone. My outer world is a reflection of my inner world. What I feel and think is what is demonstrated in my life. I am a part of an unlimited source of perfect energy; therefore I am unlimited. There are no limits to what I can have or what I can accomplish.

PAYING BILLS

Paying these bills shows the universe I have the ability to pay.
I am deeply thankful for what I have received. I do not put my
energy into resenting bills; instead I gracefully receive them
with a thankful heart. I pay these bills with love and joy. I
focus not on debt but on blessing each bill as I pay it. I am
open to the abundant flow of the universe.

Poverty Makes Me Good

My circumstances, my health, and my finances are a reflection of the ideas I carry in my head. From this day forward, I release old and negative beliefs about lack. My good comes from everywhere and through everything. My divine nature makes me a good person, not lack of money. I love being a treasured person who receives abundance from many directions. I love my abundant state!

RELUCTANCE TO GIVE MONEY AWAY

Giving keeps the flow of abundance in my life. I rejoice in the inexhaustible supply of the universe and know that giving something away leaves room for more to enter my life. I give with joy because there is enough for everyone. Keeping the flow of giving and receiving is natural and feels good. I love being part of the natural energy pattern in life. I circulate abundance!

RELUCTANCE TO SPEND MONEY

I see my bank account constantly replenished from my unlimited source. Spending money is an acknowledgment of my unlimited source. As I give and spend money, I know I receive more in surprising ways. I am open to all receiving channels. My money is always returned to me. I am a joyful giver and spender. I give and receive my lavish abundance in every area of life.

RELUCTANCE TO TIP

I love expressing my thanks by giving money to others who have given me good service. I love the gift of energy people give me. I appreciate energy gifts from other people. Recognizing a person's positive energy and good service with money keeps my abundant flow going. I attract more positive energy and good service with every tip I give.

Rich People Are Bad

I know there is enough money to go around because there is an inexhaustible, universal supply. I rejoice in the good fortune of others. I bless their fortune knowing that I am worthy of the same. We are connected to the same source and my prosperity pipeline flows to me in exactly the same way as to everyone else. I open my prosperity pipeline further, and nothing blocks the unlimited source that supplies every particle of this galaxy.

Rich People Are Snooty

I know I am a divine and whole individual; therefore I do not believe in lack. I believe in having. When others have, I rejoice in their success and know that prosperity is a state of mind that anyone is capable of having. I am receptive to having money because I deserve it, just like everyone else. I have an abundance mindset.

SALARY DEFINES ME

My salary or income is not my source. My source is my unlimited supply and the spiritual presence within me. When I embrace my source, I know I am a demonstration of unlimitedness. I transform this idea into form by always being aware of my divine composition. My source, not an amount of money, fulfills me. Feeling fulfilled interprets itself into all my experiences and in the forms I manifest. I am defined by the spirit within.

Financial Crisis

When chaos breaks out in the workplace or in your checkbook, be comforted by knowing you are not on your own. Spirit is the bank that will give you whatever you need and desire in voluminous quantities. You can count on it. Set a new mental equivalent during your temporary travel through financial adversity, and remember: you're just moving *through* it.

BAD INVESTMENTS

From this day forward, I have no need for need, lack, or loss because these thoughts are no longer present in my mind. My experiences demonstrate my own powerful thoughts. I manifest a rich and diverse life because that is what is now present in my mind. I have no need for the past or the future. In this eternal moment of now, feelings of needing, lacking, and losing are permanently stricken from my mind and body. There is an infinite supply of everything in the universe, and I am an open channel to receive. I move forward in new, prosperous directions.

CAN'T QUIT JOB BECAUSE OF FAMILY RESPONSIBILITIES

My work gives me an opportunity to tend to those I love. Right now, my calling is providing support for my family. I rejoice in my ability to give others this gift of support. I am thankful for my strength and resolve so that others can lean on me at this juncture in my life.

DIDN'T GET THE JOB

This organization is not the best place to expend my efforts. I visualize a place where I am recognized for my exceptional capabilities and paid well. There are many other organizations with people who think like me that can help me grow. I am thankful for this experience of meeting new people and know that something better is coming my way.

DISORGANIZED FINANCES

Today I walk a refreshing path of organization. I straighten my desk, throw clutter away, and clean up every area in my home and office to make room for new opportunities. My financial flow runs faster, smoother, and more efficiently without a clutter path. I now open mental and physical energy pathways for my flowing abundance. My finances reflect my mental state and I choose to be organized and precise. Being organized brings me joy and increases my prosperity in all aspects of my life.

FORCED TO MOVE HOME

Today I take time to re-evaluate what is important in my life. This experience gives me an opportunity to inventory my own perceptions of failure. I view this as a time to start anew. I now create a refreshing perspective on life. I am thankful to have a temporary refuge and thank my family today for this chance to take stock of what I want in life.

HURT PRIDE

Today I walk straight, stand tall, and hold my head up high. I am strong enough to overcome these circumstances because they are part of my own learning agenda, which I designed in my chart long before I arrived here. Every time I choose to put one foot in front of the other, I come one step closer to a new opportunity that is already here. I trust the universe to keep the wind at my back while I walk this path with strength and dignity.

LOSING THE HOUSE

This house was not meant for me to have at this time. I call my angels to come forth and place the house in a basket, and I allow them to take it away. I cover the house in a beautiful rosy light-blessing. I visualize this house already making someone else very happy. I am free from this material item in my life and feel lighter, happier, and blessed in sending it on its way.

NOT ENOUGH MONEY

My prosperity is a reflection of my consciousness. Therefore the thoughts I hold in my mind are of abundance. There is an unlimited supply of money in the universe that is constantly increasing. I deserve to prosper. I release my old, limiting ideas about lack, because I no longer believe in lack. When others have more money than I do, it takes nothing away from me because there is enough for everyone.

Pay Cut

Accepting less money for what I do gives me a chance to evaluate my creative skills. My financial loss is empty space I can fill with inventiveness. I now have an opportunity to tune up my creative thinking and find a better channel for my productivity. I deserve the best now and no longer believe in lack. I accept all good that comes my way.

RECKLESS SPENDING

My money energy is an incoming and outgoing tide. I receive my flow of money just as I engage in the flow of life. I am in a new, balanced frame of mind about my tide. All the waves are vital to the system and I treat each one with respect. I respect my money energy and keep my wave system calm and flowing regularly. I replenish my supply with ease and fluidity. From this day forward, I spend my money with an attitude of gratitude and respect.

SOLE PROVIDER

I rejoice in my ability to support this family. With each day, I become a clearer channel to provide what they need. Because of me, there are opportunities for those I love. I accept this challenge with gratitude and know that being in this position allows me to discover my inner strength.

I TAKE MY SPIRITUAL
TRUTH TO WORK EVERY
DAY AND DEMONSTRATE IT
IN EVERYTHING I DO.

Corporate Soul

Affirmations that channel
spirit and strength
into your work life

Being the Boss

Any seasoned leader will confess: with a broad range of individuals (and problems) to manage, it is difficult to arrive at our desks fresh off the philosophical freeway. We're in the reality lane the minute we check the voice messages and e-mail. Having a foothold in the spiritual realm on a moment-to-moment basis is not a subject we normally tackle in a staff debriefing when the ramifications of a lost account or a vendor relationship gone sour are on the agenda. But remember your true boss (both of them). It'll help you honor yourself and sustain you throughout the day!

BORED OWNER

I no longer use boredom as an excuse not to make the world a better place. I am action and now make changes in my life that open new channels for me to use my wisdom and experience for the greater good. I am thankful for all the people in my life who have contributed to my current success. I choose to do something for another person each day to demonstrate my thankfulness.

CAN'T FIRE EMPLOYEE

I no longer resist the structures we have set to keep our organization intact. I view this employee's presence as a lesson for me in learning how to deal with negative circumstances. I ask the universe to find a better situation for this person, one that meets their needs. I wholeheartedly surrender to this process and trust this employee is finding a place that provides nurturing in a greater capacity.

Employee with Messy Personal Life

I support my employee by surrounding them with love and light today. I visualize their tornado winding down as the dust settles. Although I protect my own energy field from a distance, I silently ask a higher power for help with these life difficulties. I feel happy knowing I have the ability to send immediate assistance to anyone I know.

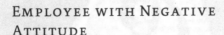

EMPLOYEE WITH NEGATIVE ATTITUDE

Today I find the courage and time to impart wisdom. I accept my responsibility in showing this person how their behavior affects others on their team. The universe helps me speak my highest truth in a loving way. This experience strengthens me and benefits others in our organization and the world.

ENERGY LAMPREYS

I recognize that this person feeds off my energy field, and this drains me. I cannot provide my service to the world without a full cup of energy. Today I am protected with self-love and use my own energy for the greater good. My cup is full. I no longer feel responsible for completing this person. This person is responsible for their own happiness.

Feeling like Mother-Manager

I already nurture my staff at a spiritual level. My ability to hold strong in a chaotic work environment is the best example I can give my staff. I ask that every difficult employee be filled with the powerful guidance of the divine mother. I am thankful that my presence is viewed as an inspiration to others.

FISCALLY IRRESPONSIBLE EMPLOYEE

Today I lovingly honor those who are working hard in this organization by preventing more waste. Although there is abundance on this planet, we must utilize our resources wisely, out of respect for nature and humanity. Today I take action to change this situation because others are relying upon me to show my deep honor. I am courageous in my methods and strongly step up to my task with resolve.

MANAGEMENT TEAM STAGNATING

My team is a river and I can inspire them to keep moving forward. The sea holds a multitude of ideas and opportunities; it is where the creative juice flows. Our organization has all the tools to be successful and I am one of them. I visualize my team moving with renewed vigor and enthusiasm.

MEETINGS NOT PRODUCTIVE

Our creative energy falls through a sieve because we are undisciplined in our thinking and preparation. Today I encourage my team to center themselves before our meeting and wear a new attitude of respect for one another. When our souls recognize one another in an area of loving respect, a new level of creative energy transpires. I appreciate everyone on my team for challenging my ability to provide focus.

MOVING THE OFFICE

I rejoice in the opportunity to find a new place to grow. The prospect of new surroundings is already facilitating creative ideas. I anticipate this move with excitement about the new possibilities for our organization. I feel a breath of fresh air move through me and inspire my thinking.

OVERWORK

I am overworked because I choose to be out of balance. Today I begin a course of action that aligns my work schedule with healthy living. From this day forward, I am committed to balancing my work and personal life. I am created from an image of balance.

PREPARING TO FIRE EMPLOYEE

I ask for divine guidance in sending this person off to a situation that better meets their needs. I allow this person to leave with grace and dignity. I gratefully acknowledge being part of a relationship consisting of two souls who have met on their learning journeys. Today I am thankful for what I have learned, both as an employer and as a magnanimous individual.

STAFF NOT SUPPORTIVE

Today I find the source of negativity in my staff. While I remove those who do not share this organization's vision, I also examine my own behavior and management style. I address this needed balance in my work situation with a renewed sense of vigor. I have a positive attitude focused on improvement.

STARING INTO THE ABYSS

I have come this far and there's no turning back. I face my challenges head on and know this is the time for me to believe in who I am and what I can do. I ask spirit to help guide me to make the best decisions. I now rely on intuition, not logic, and I am grateful for knowing the value of both.

STARTING A NEW BUSINESS

My independent spirit knows no boundaries. I have grown tall enough to stand with others who think the way I do. Perfect order is at work in my life and allows me to solve my problems. The universe leads me into my groove. As I unfold, my business unfolds. It is a loving venture and adventure.

UNGRATEFUL EMPLOYEES

Like a mother's work, the work I do daily does not always translate into visible results. I know results are present every day and I ask the Divine to assist me to see clearly. The energy I give my employees is like a bank deposit from which they draw when it's needed. My energy is a gift and I am thankful for the opportunity to help others step into a higher vision.

Uninspired Team

People depend upon me to be an example of leadership and integrity. My actions illustrate my strong beliefs in this organization and its potential. I believe each person on my team is a leader and inspires others. I adjust my channel to direct their energy more productively for the benefit of those who are working hard in this organization.

Whiny Employees

My employees need to step into a vision of their own brilliance. I visualize lifting them higher, where they can see themselves and their own words more clearly. I surround them with love and silently ask that they speak their highest spiritual truth. I now redirect my own energy to purposes that are for the greater good. I trust the universal order to put my energy in the best place.

Co-Workers

I've often pondered why it's so darn hard to get along with co-workers. Like many of you, I've sprinkled my entrepreneurial years with theory: TQM, collective leadership, W. Edwards Deming, quality circles, paradigm shifts, koans, and learning organization principles. I've decided we're making it just too complicated. We're driving ourselves nuts and afraid to say what the act of work really means. It's a spiritual practice, where the basics are service to others, compassion, forgiveness, generosity, gratitude. These should be given in big doses – even to the grumpy receptionist who won't share the bathroom code when you forget.

COMPETING FOR POWER

The law of physics is on my side; therefore, to achieve success, I choose to let go. By letting go, I learn to surrender to the universe with trust. Through surrender, I flow to success and new possibilities. I am no longer paddling upstream; I am relaxed in my current and enjoying the view. My divine gifts are appreciated by others.

COMPLAINTS ABOUT ME

My situation takes me to a state of higher awareness. I take my lumps today and use the complaints as an opportunity to improve. This situation already serves me well because I have a better idea of who I am. I am divine substance, and I stand tall in the face of adversity.

CO-WORKER EMOTIONALLY
DEPENDENT ON ME

This co-worker has not realized their potential because they do not see their capabilities. I visualize their body, heart, and mind filled with the light of self-realization. I am not responsible for their happiness. I facilitate their spiritual path by releasing them to the perfect order of the universe.

DEFENSIVE BEHAVIOR

Today I become more approachable and loving, both inside and outside my work environment. Although I acknowledge that some people do not handle criticism well, I can still improve my ability to communicate and to compliment others. I am thankful for this opportunity to fine-tune my own behavior, and I know it will make me more successful in all areas of my life.

DIFFICULT PERSONALITIES

The people in my work environment are showing me areas in my own work behavior that are lacking. I welcome the opportunity for self-improvement by carefully looking at my own behavior and reactions. I put a positive light of love around my co-workers and bless them in their own learning journey and also for enhancing mine.

FIRED CO-WORKER

I surround my co-worker with love and visualize their success. I choose to work in the present moment and re-examine my own purpose in this organization. I thank the universe for giving me an opportunity to show compassion. This experience gives me a chance to realign my goals with those of my organization.

GOSSIP

Today I visualize my co-workers speaking their highest spiritual truth. I imagine a purple light around their mouths. I visualize their spoken words having the highest vibration. I am impervious to hurtful words because I am protected by my aura of goodness. Like water off a duck's back, this gossip slides away. I am completely detached from hurtful gossip.

LACK OF COMPASSION AMONG
TEAM MEMBERS

The lack of compassion I observe among my co-workers is a direct result of compassion lacking in my own personal life. From this day forward, I vow to reach out and view other people's lives as they see them. I have the strength and ability to be a role model for those who are currently lacking in compassion. I am the ambassador of compassion in my workplace.

OVER-INVOLVEMENT IN A
CO-WORKER'S PERSONAL LIFE

I am interfering with this person's ability to grow. I now allow this person to experience the lessons they have chosen on their own soul journey. I release my influence on them in a loving way and ask that a higher power surround them with assistance. I believe that this person's life lessons are meant for their own self-development.

POOR WORK ETHIC

It doesn't matter if others do not work as hard as I do. Working hard is not an expectation others place on me: I choose to work hard because I believe in my calling and cause. The best way I can inspire others is to lead by example, not by criticism. I am mindful of my health and, from this day forward, make a commitment to balancing work and play.

SHARING MY TURF

I imagine my heart growing bigger today. I allow others to share in what I already have and know. My light becomes brighter when I open the aperture of my heart. Others are not a threat to me; they only enhance my light. I welcome the opportunity to be a teacher and share what I have learned.

SNIPPY WOMEN

I am a warrior against negativity. I am a soldier armed with positive energy and love. Every belittling word I hear I deflect with my shield of maturity and rise to a higher plateau of resilience. I ask the universe to allow me to speak my highest spiritual truth and inspire others to do the same.

STABBED IN THE BACK

Some people in life enjoy hurting others through either intention or ignorance. Today I heal my wounds by loving myself even more than I did yesterday. Divine light fills my wound until there is nothing but joy inside me. I am unafraid to continue to show the world who I am. I am blessed with strength and fortitude.

TEAM MEMBER DISCOURAGING OTHERS

I have an intuitive ability to channel the positive energy of others on my team. Although many believe we have hurdles too high to overcome, I know we are not alone in what needs to be done. I ask the universe to assist me in raising my energy level. I am a continual positive influence on others on my team. People look to me because they know I am strong. I do not allow small setbacks to discourage those who depend upon me for strength.

TEAM MEMBER NOT PULLING WEIGHT

There are times when we must expand our hearts to help others. I release my resentment over this situation and focus energy on my own performance. This is a good time for me to learn how to put my efforts into meeting a goal. I am capable of temporarily expanding my presence in order to fill the space this person leaves. I am a valuable asset to this organization.

Employees

As an employee, it is important for you to have the confidence to carry out a vision. Good leadership, which makes great organizations, always likes to align people with a high ideal. Word your résumé as if you are already walking on the path to success, and be proud of what you have done. Go for the honest cover letter. Employers love inquisitive minds who view work as a course-altering event. They know employees who have positive attitudes about what they learned from their last job will spread positive energy when the going gets rough. Remember, you are building form with idea, both within and outside your workplace! Know that you have an opportunity to demonstrate your true self at work. Affirm the higher power within!

ASKING FOR A RAISE

My talents have grown to a point where I require balance between energy expended and reward. I have inventoried the reasons why the imbalance exists between what I do and my financial compensation for doing it. I look forward to expressing those reasons out loud because it allows me an opportunity to see my energy equation more clearly.

Boss Is Never Satisfied

My employer is unable to recognize my potential because they cannot see their own potential. Working for this person is teaching me to stretch the limits of my own image and imagination. I am a competent individual with a lot to offer this organization. I am proud of my strong and competent self.

Bringing Personal Strife to Work

Today I set sail on a more disciplined course of action to inspire others in this organization. My greatest contribution is showing others how well I can weather the storm. I resolve to bring a higher level of awareness to those around me as I set a positive example of how to manage life's difficulties. My heart and mind are strong. All is well in the world.

FEELING LIKE A NUMBER IN A LARGE ORGANIZATION

Every person on this planet, every soul is a unique spark of the Divine. My contribution is important because no one has my unique essence. I contribute to the greater good through this organization because I am a vital element of the universe. My presence is a gift to others.

IDEAS REJECTED

Even though my ideas express the essence of me, I stand strong when my creativity is rejected. I am being focused by spirit to improve the quality of my work; therefore I joyfully look forward to fine-tuning my ideas. My ideas are already reaching a big audience. I am a visionary and far ahead of my time. I am a creative thinker and people welcome my point of view with love and open arms.

Inadequate Pay

I make a beautiful contribution to this organization, and that translates into a higher salary. Starting today, I am showcasing my special talents that deserve to be rewarded. Every word I speak inspires others to reward me. I am worthy and love what I do! I deserve to be rewarded for what I do. I love feeling worthy.

Job Is Not Challenging

My position is a step leading toward greater satisfaction. I am thankful to the universe for the time I can spend to choose my next course of action carefully. There is another job where I will shine and my efforts will benefit others. I welcome change in my life, love change, and become more flexible each day.

JOB IS NOT MY TRUE CALLING

Finding the path for my soul work is a journey. I am a work in progress. My current work is a path leading to higher ground. There is a better place where my expertise is recognized. I now release my attachment to this job to provide space in my life for new growth. I accept the learning that arrives from this experience and know that it shapes me into a stronger and smarter individual.

JOB UNDERUTILIZES MY TALENTS

This position is only a stopping point in my life. I am a smart, wonderful, fantastic person with a lot of expertise to offer the world! I place my energy in areas that allow me to showcase my talents. At this moment, I am attracting people into my life who recognize my unlimited capabilities. I am now flowing to a new place with unlimited opportunities.

New Boss

In order for me to grow, change is necessary. I am creating a new energy pattern in my organization by visualizing a new person who recognizes my unique capabilities. This experience gives me an opportunity for self-examination. I put my own mental and emotional energies in order. I am in tune with the complete order and logic of the universe as an expression of my dual creation.

Not Enough Time to Do Job Well

I am the ambassador of quality. The service I provide for others is recognized for its quality and attention to detail. I resist the urge to judge my own performance and focus on doing my job with loving intention. I am proud of my quality service because I know it is a reflection of me.

REQUEST FOR RAISE REFUSED

My employer is not my source. My job is not my source. The true source of my supply is the unlimited, inexhaustible supply of the Divine. I open my channels to my supply and do not limit my supply by looking to others who are not my source. I flow easily and fluidly with my vision of the Divine.

Organizations

Even when negotiating sticky vendor relationships and dealing with the unsavory aspects of business, such as firings or getting sued, we want everyone to win. Although winning is a value, don't let it get in the way of the big picture. Work requires *huge* perspective and, of course, the practice of positively affirming that it's all for our higher good anyway. Find equilibrium between your warrior and your goddess – your reason for being in business in the first place – and use your emotions to keep the warrior spirit in check.

DECLINING SALES

My ability to convince someone to buy our product or service is a direct result of my belief in it. I now realign my energy with that of my product or service, and know deeply that it is meant to facilitate a better life for humanity. No matter what others say, I am helping the world to be a better place. I am not a salesperson; I am an ambassador for the greater good.

GROWING THE BUSINESS

There is a wealth of abundance on this planet, available to everyone. I rejoice in my abundance and am thankful that I can demonstrate it in the form of my business. Like a child, my organization has growing pains. I welcome this part of the process because it expands my overall perspective. My organization is already part of the abundant framework of life.

LOSING MONEY

This organization has everything it needs to be successful. I contribute to this organization's prosperity by knowing I already have everything. While waiting for this organization to come into perfect alignment with a vision of success held by many, I concentrate on being a magnet for prosperity in every aspect of my life. I am richly abundant, with all I need. My abundance at work is a reflection of my personal prosperity consciousness.

Myopic Management

I visualize this organization wearing prescription glasses. The management team is capable of seeing clearly. Part of my soul work is to contribute to a clearer vision of what this organization can do. I assist people at the highest level of this organization by helping them see clearly.

ORGANIZATION CHANGING HANDS

There is no transformation without chaos. Complete renewal is brought about by stirring the pot. Being in the center of chaos allows me to question what I do for a living and determine whether I am ready for personal transformation, by my own hand. During this time of uncertainty, I determine whether this work environment allows me to express my true nature. I am confident in my abilities!

REALIGNING ORGANIZATIONAL GOALS

I have the ability to direct my team and rechannel their energies. My purpose today is to inspire them to harness their desire for success for the good of everyone in this organization. I intend to inspire them to step up to a higher level of responsibility for the good of others. I am strong and determined!

SELLING THE BUSINESS

I have led the people in my organization as far as I can on their learning journey. I ask for guidance in releasing this relationship for the benefit of all involved. Everyone in the organization is now on a happier path toward their own self-development. I am already on a new adventure where my capabilities are being utilized in other areas of my life and the larger human community.

STAGNATION

My organization is a pool of still water and I am responsible for stimulating movement. I can revitalize this organization. It takes only one drop of water to create movement, and I am that drop. My contribution has far-reaching effects, no matter how small others perceive it to be.

Ungrateful Management Team

I choose to release my work frustrations in the form of a productive physical activity. If those at the highest level of this organization squander their opportunities, it does not affect me. What I do not like in others may mirror my own intentions; therefore I examine my own behavior for faulty thinking. I am thankful for my success and I ask for divine guidance in bringing this situation into balance.

Workplace Crisis

Workplace crisis makes us want to forget about stepping up to the plate: it's easier to ignore the pitch and run for cover. But if we view crisis as the necessary dynamic principle required to stimulate positive change, we can get through it because change is the natural order of things. Never be fearful of success or failure. You are not defined by money, your job, or anything but your source, the ultimate coach who knows you are a winner no matter what.

Discrimination

I have experienced discrimination because others are unwilling to let their soul recognize my soul. We are all composed of the same perfect substance. I forgive others for their lack of insight and know that this experience is meant to show me a part of the human condition. I am a beloved and unique individual who is empowered by divine love and light.

Downsizing

This organization must take in energy more efficiently in order to transform it into something that benefits the greater good. I am part of a soul plan that is about growth through transformation. My presence here is a positive contribution to ordering the world.

Equipment Breakdown

I view this delay as a chance to reset my priorities today. This interruption frees me to breathe. Although I can continue to work, it is a sign that something goes unchecked. I take a moment to quietly reboot my thought process. All is well in the world.

FEMALE OPPRESSION

I am filled with the power of Mother God today. I am a universal web of connectivity with every life-form on this planet. I am the cycle of life, death, and rebirth, which is an eternal energy pattern. My presence is powerful, loving, and here to stay.

LEGAL ACTION AGAINST ME

This experience is difficult but also gives me clarity. I face my actions truthfully and ask the universe to give me courage to speak my highest spiritual truth. This experience is an opportunity to allow others to question what I have done. I stand strong in my personal beliefs.

LEGAL ACTION AGAINST
SOMEONE ELSE

This lawsuit is a consequence of standing up for what I believe in. I am supported in my efforts to speak the truth and bring truth to others. I believe my intentions are pure and my actions were taken for the right reasons. I know that divine order is at work in my life. I am supported by a divine super-structure of universal justice.

UNETHICAL REQUESTS

My heart tells me what is right and wrong, and my mind knows the difference. I am joyful in my ability to choose the right path. Each choice in my life permits me to grow as an individual, no matter the outcome. I am blessed by my creator because I have a choice in how I utilize my gifts. I am unencumbered by what people think because my heart leads the way.

Unscrupulous Organization

My work does not allow me to illuminate the world, where I can be of service. Therefore I release my gifts to others outside this organization and ask for assistance in finding the right channel for the greater good. My new job is in alignment with my higher ideals. I now travel a path with others who have a strong commitment to improving the world.

As I search for divine love, I find it inside myself. My understanding and acceptance of love makes my light shine brighter. I am supported by a higher power in every aspect of my life.

The Divine Feminine

Affirmations for the
Goddess in you

I AM Everywhere

When you finally release all fears, you begin to live life as a prayer. Remember that fears are the reason it may take us so long to succeed. Get rid of fears and you'll have no emotional and mental clutter, leaving room to become a channel of higher power. You'll be able to open yourself to the journey of becoming who you really are and invite more of what you want in your life. Infinite wisdom is at work in your life, whether you're picking socks up off the floor or speaking on the dais. Revisit the Divine within often! You are a channel of the Divine, both He and She, in everything you do.

Bringing My Gifts to the World

I know my energy is needed in more ways than I can imagine. When I offer my sacred self to others and engage in my soul work, I become part of a timeless, universal equation that knows no boundaries. I help to evolve my God-self, resulting in complete transformation of consciousness. I am significant and feel proud knowing that, within all things, I am the air, the love, and the thought of the Divine, who creates through me.

CONSCIOUSNESS OF THE HOLY SPIRIT

The Holy Spirit is love expressed between Mother and Father God. When I am consciously aware of the love between intellect and emotion, I am immersed in spirit. I allow spirit to enter my mind and heart so that I may express it in my actions. I am filled with spirit. I am an expression of Christ consciousness (or Buddha, or other spiritual leaders) when I am in a state of self-awareness of the Holy Spirit.

CONSCIOUSNESS OF SELF

My true self is the universal consciousness and is all that is. Consciousness is the web, the interconnectivity, and the superstructure, and I am a manifestation of the Divine. My true self is composed of pure light and energy. I am consciousness and unconsciousness, and I am the absolute mystery. My purpose is to gain more knowledge of my true self.

DEMONSTRATING SPIRIT IN MY WORK

My work is an authentic self-expression. When I know I am my God-self, my work becomes a sacred expression of the Mother, the Father, and Christ consciousness within. My soul evolves through the work I do; therefore I have a distinct purpose that is unique to me. I facilitate everyone's self-development through the work I do.

FEELING AS IF THE WORLD WILL END

This planetary realm seems negative, but I join forces with others who want to overcome the darkness. There is work to be done on earth. As long as I exist in this body, I can work toward improving the human condition. I focus my energies on improvement through loving intentions and create a beautiful physical world. With every breath I take, I inhale light, not darkness, to demonstrate love and create goodness. The world needs my positive contribution!

FEELING PART OF A TRIUNE

I am consciously aware of my existence. I exist within Mother God, Father God, and the Holy Spirit that is demonstrated on earth. I am capable of demonstrating Christ consciousness in my life. I am a spark of the Divine, and I exist in an eternal state with my divine parents; therefore I am a demonstration of the triune. I am He, She, and the Christ. I become one with the All as I accept the Divine within me. I am empowered by knowing I am spirit.

FEELING PART OF A UNIVERSAL PLAN

I chose this incarnation because I have important work to do. My contribution is needed, because my presence fills a unique space in consciousness. My energy is needed to evolve the world. Because I am needed, I am irreplaceable. I receive thanks in the form of a self-development opportunity. I evolve as the creator evolves, making my presence here valuable, irreplaceable, and needed in the universe.

THE GODDESS IS EVERYWHERE

My blessed Mother, my Goddess, I see you in all. You move energy from the unmanifest to the manifest. Your presence is sacred on earth. I am part of your fabric and I weave my world into yours, as my life is an exercise in what I create as well as what you create through me. Because I belong to you, my life is filled with meaning. I am alive with purpose. Every word I speak, everywhere I look, there is you: your wisdom, your harmony, your cycle, your transformative power.

LOVING MOTHER GOD

I love my Mother as I love my God-self. There are no boundaries for love, because it is composed of infinite spirit. Loving Her makes me connect with both what I see and what I do not. My heart safely beats with hers. Great Mother of Heaven, let me know I am with you in spirit, as I am a part of you. I make room for the Mother as I have done for the Father, and embracing both makes my loving self-image complete.

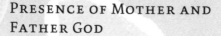

PRESENCE OF MOTHER AND FATHER GOD

I awake to the presence within to become whole. I am spirit. My Father holds all constant; my Mother is sacred as She is intellect demonstrated. She is within me, as is He. Since my power comes from both, and as I realize they are All that is, I am empowered by my God-self. I exist knowing my Mother and Father bless me in every effort I make to create a better world for others to live in.

SEEING SPIRIT EVERYWHERE

If I create distance from God/Goddess, I cannot feel my power fully. My power comes from within, because spirit is uncontained. At this moment, I allow spirit to pervade my thoughts and intentions. We are spirit manifest. Spirit recognizes spirit; therefore we have an opportunity to recognize the Divine in one another. From this day forward, I choose to see spirit in everyone and everything within my purview. I love my authentic self as I love others.

Loving Spirit

Whether we admit it or not, if we don't identify with something that gives us a sense of power, there's not much to fall back on when the going gets rough. Loving spirit, no matter how you label it, is the entire foundation of positive thinking. It is the act of loving the essence of *you*. When you generate enough love to love yourself fully and without inhibition, you'll feel worthy. You won't need to patch up your psyche with plastic surgery, exercise, or addictions, or by blaming your parents, the weather, or the company that didn't hire you. Have a love festival with your authentic self, who is magnificent, and appreciate every quirk. Your spirit is the swan awaiting its reveal.

CAN'T FIND A PLACE TO WORSHIP

My temple is in my heart. No matter where I go or what I do, my actions and thoughts are a prayer. My words are a loving dedication to spirit. My presence on earth is a tribute to the Divine within me; therefore in everything I do, everywhere I go, I am in a worshipful place. My church is everywhere.

RECOGNIZING SPIRIT

I now align with my God-self and know that my own consciousness belongs to everyone on this planet. All life contains spirit and I am a reflection of the Divine. I am He, I am She, and they are within me. Together we are unified as one presence, one blessing, and one light.

SEEING RESULTS FROM PRAYER

My prayers are always heard and answered in universal time. My results reflect the clarity of intention. I am an observer of my role in the universe. I am a co-creator with the Divine, knowing I do half the work by believing in my earth self and my divine self. I can do anything I set my mind and heart to, and at this moment I align my intentions with those for the greater good, knowing as I pray that I have already received everything I have asked for.

SEEKING A SPIRITUAL EXCHANGE

No matter what I do, I am part of spirit. The language of spirit is both intellect and emotion; therefore what I think and do is an expression of spirit. I choose to channel spirit through a beautiful and productive medium that is for the greater good. As I walk this planet, I am speaking to spirit because I am the channel and the medium; divine wisdom is my infrastructure. I dance to an endless and dynamic spiritual tempo.

SEEKING UNIVERSAL LOVE

At this moment, I strip away all the accoutrements of earth life, my body, and all concern. I exist in the light of my true nature, which is my God-self. My heart opens, knowing that the Divine is manifest in each of us on this planet. My life is a sacred act; therefore I live the act of love in all I do. There is opportunity for me to magnify the expression of love, which is inherent in each of us. I am a full expression of love through my words and actions.

VISIONARY IN THE WRONG TIME AND PLACE

I am light-years beyond the norm. Since I fit perfectly with other visionaries of my time, I am in perfect company. I exist simultaneously in the past, the present, and the future because time is an infinite continuum. My timelessness makes me belong anywhere, anyplace, and I love my place. I am a moment in time, right for my time, and an idea whose time has come. I accept the timing of Mother and Father God.

Loving Your Complete Self

At some point, you'll need to shed all your reasons for not believing you are an incredible individual and just put your authentic self on autopilot. Although everyone likes validation from outside sources, we actually find happiness and comfort when we identify with an image of divine perfection. Your authentic self *is* perfect. Even when everyday negative happenstance may prod you to self-doubt, there should be no reason to block your own success. You can't let downbeat messages from others translate into worries about what you are capable of doing. If that happens, you have confused your ego with your true self, settling on a definition of success that has nothing to do with who you are and everything to do with external circumstances. Listen to your voice from within instead of Aunt Edna, who will never like your pot roast no matter what you do. Stand up, be strong, and learn to identify with spirit. See yourself in the Divine!

ALTERNATIVE LIFESTYLES AND SELF-LOVE

No matter how different my lifestyle, I know I am loved by a higher power. My true self is the same God-self that exists within every human on this planet. I am now and will always be part of a family of souls whose light shines bright. I love myself for who I am. I honor the Divine by loving my authentic self.

BELIEF IN WHAT I CAN DO

Believing in myself is the same as believing in the Divine, because I am a spark of the Divine. No matter the setbacks, I know I walk a path of self-discovery. Each step on my path brings me closer to the Divine. I remain strong despite adversity, negativity, and rejection, which only increase my endurance. I am a warrior for Mother and Father God. By believing in what I can do, I honor my authentic self as I honor them.

Can't Find My Gift to the World

Today my perspective widens as I continue on my lifetime learning journey. I am thankful for the opportunity to self-develop by walking many avenues. I was born with purpose. I trust that I already inspire others on their path each day. Divine guidance clarifies my purpose so that I can achieve greater understanding of my gifts. I am already a tremendous gift to everyone in my life!

FEELING I AM NOT GOOD ENOUGH

I make a fabulous contribution to the universe in the form of my exceptional gifts. I am just right exactly the way I am, which is my authentic self. I choose not to follow anyone's expectations of me. I sing my own music! Since I operate on my own frequency, my song is beautiful and strong and will be right for those who are attuned to what I sing.

MAKING CHANGES FOR OTHERS

I find my center in the complexity of life where the voice of spirit speaks to me. Together, we view my circumstances objectively in order to determine where I need to make change. When I choose to change, I do it from my power center and change for me, not because others tell me to. My change comes from a joyful place that keeps me on the path to self-development.

RECOGNIZING MY OWN DIVINITY

I am the light that has found expression in what is manifest on earth. I am both transcendent and immanent. I am consciousness that seeks an answer to the meaning of self. By being present on earth, I help solve the eternal mystery. I am divine energy because I belong to the eternal and universal self, which is God and Goddess. We are all the universe, and the universe is me, the Divine is in me, spirit is in me, and I am composed of spirit, in an infinite pattern of light, an all-knowing web of love. I open my heart to receiving grace from who I am, which is love and light, me everywhere. In all things my living, infinite spirit exists.

SELF-LOVE: FEMALE QUALITIES

I love being female. I am all seasons, all cycles, all elements. Each breath I take is prayer as I connect with Mother Earth, the great primordial womb. I see the Goddess in me now and view the past with love. I am lovable and worthy of love because I already exist in a symbiotic state of love with Mother God. As I occupy my body of earth-femaleness, I walk with Her in loving harmony.

SELF-LOVE: MALE QUALITIES

My male qualities balance my female qualities. I love my two distinct energies, which cannot exist without each other. My masculine side brings order but cradles my feminine side, and my feminine side embraces and gives birth to my masculine side. I am both parts of Mother and Father God, whose arms are in an eternal, loving embrace.

SELF-LOVE IN THE FACE OF REJECTION

I deeply internalize the essence of forgiveness and compassion when I am rejected. I am learning to be balanced despite my circumstances. Even though others reject my human expressions, they improve my ability to love myself. My self-love knows no boundaries because I can love in the face of chaos. I am empowered by my state of self-love!

ACKNOWLEDGMENTS

I would like to express my gratitude to my husband, Tom, who has encouraged me to do my soul work for the Goddess. Tom, you have given me your own rendition of a King Air, in the form of creative freedom. Your life has been a gift. Special thanks to my agent, Arnold Gosewich; the entire staff at Cattails; my editor, Barbara Czarnecki; and Linda Gustafson and Peter Ross at Counterpunch. And of course, to my circle at The Goddess Network, thanks for all you do and especially for the very special and positive energies that you gave to this project. To everyone who participates in our online community at www.thegoddess network.net, I thank you for sharing your stories. You are the reason we keep going. Deepest thanks to all my vendors who have provided good humor, great service, plenty of coffee, and dedication over the years. I believe we are together for a reason.

You have all been a blessing in my life and I continue to grow because of you.

About the Author

Charlene M. Proctor holds a Doctor of Philosophy degree from the University of Michigan and provides guidance through everyday complexity with female imagery and positive thinking. She is the founder of The Goddess Network, Inc., an organization for women who want to discover the feminine principle within. Her lectures, workshops, and electronic programs reach a worldwide audience daily. Although Charlene has written numerous papers on the subject of simulation, organizational learning, and recycling technologies, her material for a wider audience gives her the greatest pleasure. *Let Your Goddess Grow! 7 Spiritual Lessons on Female Power and Positive Thinking* and *The Women's Book of Empowerment: 323 Affirmations That Change Everyday Problems into Moments of Potential* are her two current works. She lives with her husband and two teenage boys in the Detroit metropolitan area.

About the Goddess Network Press

The Goddess Network Press publishes books on the Goddess, spirituality, personal growth, women's issues, simulation and learning environments, and positive thinking. We hope to make a difference in the lives of those who write books, as well as for our readers. Of course, we are in love with the Goddess and see our publishing company helping to spread divine feminine energy around the globe.

We believe everything on earth is a reflection of what is inside our heads. Our challenge in life is to allow our divine nature to work with ideas that make sense. A balanced world will be created by individuals who understand and embrace their true self.

As a member of the business community, The Goddess Network, Inc. is a venue for both live and electronic gatherings for anyone interested in expanding their intellectual and spiritual boundaries, especially women who want to nurture their spirit. We promote programs that foster deeper meaning and purpose in an individual's life.

Thanks for being our reader. We value your input and suggestions on this book and on others you would like to see published. Why not contact us? We are only an e-mail away.

The Goddess Network Press
233 Pierce Street
Birmingham, Michigan
48009 USA
toll free: 866-888-04633
tel: 248-642-1300
fax: 248-642-1700
e-mail: tgn@thegoddessnetwork.net
www.thegoddessnetwork.net

The Goddess Network On-line

* Send a free e-soul card!
* Register for *Divine Woman*, our free e-newsletter
* Join Forget Me Not™
* Participate in an on-line forum
* Visit our She Shop!
* Send an e-power thought
* View our movie *A Visit with the Divine Mother*
* Madame Pele's Bookclub
* Guest columnists
* See our Goddess Values
* Register for Charlene's live programs and lectures

LET YOUR GODDESS GROW!

7 Spiritual Lessons on Female Power and Positive Thinking

" Charlene M. Proctor speaks
her mind about life, strife, and
what we need to overcome the
odds. These times demand a
more creative outlook on life
by reaching beyond current
intellectual boundaries. Readers
will love this spiritual tune-up
on why we ought to be heading
toward Goddess wisdom."

Lynn A. Robinson, author of
Divine Intuition and
Real Prosperity

Let Your Goddess Grow!
7 Spiritual Lessons on Female Power
and Positive Thinking

US $24.95 CAN   0-9766012-0-6

lable from The Goddess Network,

66-888-4633!

egoddessnetwork.net